Frank Clifford is one of Britain's leading astrologe[...]
predict the future with accuracy has attracted so[...]
names in the worlds of showbiz and sport. In add[...]
teaching seminars and contributing to radio and t[...]
own highly successful astro-palmistry practice in [...]

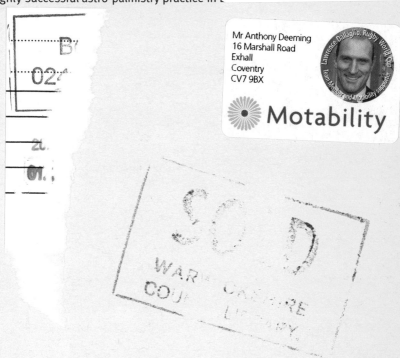

By the same author:

British Entertainers: The Astrological Profiles
The Essentials of Hand Analysis
Venus: Your Key to Love
Mars: Your Burning Desires

PALMISTRY 4 TODAY

The Fast and Accurate Way to Understand Yourself and the People Around You

Frank C. Clifford

RIDER
LONDON · SYDNEY · AUCKLAND · JOHANNESBURG

1 3 5 7 9 10 8 6 4 2

First published in 2002 by Rider,
an imprint of Ebury Press, Random House,
20 Vauxhall Bridge Road, London SW1V 2SA

Random House Australia (Pty) Limited
20 Alfred Street, Milsons Point, Sydney, New South Wales 2061, Australia

Random House New Zealand Limited
18 Poland Road, Glenfield, Auckland 10, New Zealand

Random House South Africa (Pty) Limited
Endulini, 5A Jubilee Road, Parktown 2193, South Africa

The Random House Group Limited Reg. No. 954009

Papers used by Rider are natural, recyclable products made from wood grown in
sustainable forests.

Printed and bound by Mackays of Chatham plc, Kent

Line illustrations by Malcolm Wright
Designed by Jerry Goldie Graphic Design

A CIP catalogue record for this book
is available from the British Library

ISBN 0-7126-1584-9

Note from the Publisher: the hand analysis and health diagnosis information in
this book is not intended to be taken as a replacement for professional medical
advice. Any person with a condition requiring medical attention should consult a
qualified practitioner or therapist.

Contents

Acknowledgements

My sincere thanks to Julia McCutchen for believing in this book from the beginning; to Sue Lascelles, Jerry Goldie and the team at Rider for their support and guidance; to my agents Doreen Montgomery and Caroline Montgomery; to Sue Tompkins for putting me in touch; to Malcolm Wright for his generosity and excellent artwork; to Sally Fry who first ignited my interest in palmistry and taught me so much; to my supportive parents and Helen, Filly and Nico; and all the clients, friends and 'guinea pigs' who allowed me to use their palm prints and relate their stories.

To Roberto, who has changed my life

Preface

You can blame my unusual, somewhat provocative profession on my mother! I grew up fascinated by her stories of the clairvoyants and the palm readers she and her friends visited. Some readings were a waste of time (the readers would dish out the same rubbish to every client who walked in) or of money (the only 'loss' successfully foretold being the consultant's fee). But a few readings – the occasional few – were on the money. One reader in particular spoke of fascinating twists of fate for my mother and her friends: a foreign marriage, an adoption, a car accident. His stories were dismissed – even laughed at – until, one by one, the predictions came true.

My fascination with these matters (and no doubt an unconscious need to understand myself better) led to me deciding to take a trip to a clairvoyant at the age of 15. A visit to an astrologer a while later led to the decision to begin teaching myself astrology that same afternoon. How difficult could it really be? Astrology, and the desire to spend countless hours studying birth charts, grew into a passion that remains today, but by the age of 17 I was looking for more answers and so I visited a palm reader.

I soon found that palmistry was very different from astrology, although they both backed each other consistently up. I began to study both subjects, and when I left home for university my knowledge proved to be my greatest ally in making new friends. I found palmistry's immediacy a great advantage, and I was sure that it could never be watered down by the generalities of newspaper columns. It is simply too personal, too one-to-one. People sense an untold mystery about the subject too. I continued to study books on the subject as well as read the hands of hundreds of students and friends. At one stage I even had the audacity to teach the subject at evening classes at the university. Perhaps it was the 'Teacher's Square' on both my hands that led me to lecture on a subject I had studied for all of five minutes. However, I was determined to learn by trial and error, listening to people's life stories and looking for a correlation in their

Palm Print 1
The various palm lines explained in Palmistry 4 Today

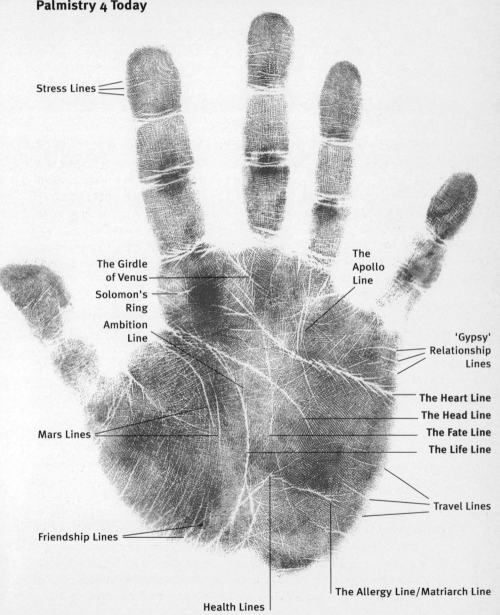

Stress Lines

The Girdle of Venus

Solomon's Ring

Ambition Line

The Apollo Line

'Gypsy' Relationship Lines

The Heart Line

The Head Line

The Fate Line

The Life Line

Mars Lines

Travel Lines

Friendship Lines

The Allergy Line/Matriarch Line

Health Lines

hands. It still amazes me that – even in my teenage years – people would tell me the most personal matters. Clients twice my age would divulge secrets, explain intimate problems and proclivities, and seek help in many other areas.

All this work led to what I do now: astro-palmistry. I write books and articles, as well as teach and consult, on both astrology and palmistry. It really is a job like no other. I love it. I'm still intrigued by the secrets that appear in our hands, and I think you'll love learning about the secrets of palmistry too.

Frank C. Clifford

Introduction

Nowadays we demand that everything be instant, accessible, comprehensive and comprehensible. We can thank the world-wide web, faxes, digital TV and increasing technical wizardry with the old-fashioned telephone for making the world seem so small. Yet it still takes the same time to experience life's important events: getting to know someone, falling in love, losing a loved one. People still need – and seek – help and advice on these matters. This is where the ancient study of palmistry, or hand analysis as it is sometimes now described, can be especially relevant.

Our attitude to life's significant happenings may not have changed over the centuries, but people today need a fresh and less deterministic perspective from esoteric disciplines such as palmistry. This book aims to provide an up-to-date approach to life's experiences using the more sophisticated techniques of modern hand analysis.

What Palmistry Can Do for Us

Palmistry can provide us with clear insights into our innate character, our needs and wants, and our attitudes to our current circumstances. It can help us to diagnose recurring problems in relationships, uncover the expectations of others and recognise the destructive roles we often assume. It can reassure us about our talents, our life challenges and opportunities. However, palmists cannot (unlike some reputable psychics) furnish us with accurate names and details of places and people coming into our lives.

A study of the hand enables us to focus on the important aspects of our lives that we can change. Our hands are living symbols of our lives and our attitudes as they currently stand. Rather than revealing a fixed pattern – an unalterable destiny – our hands impart substantial information about our temperament, personality, motivations and methods.

By interpreting the language of the hand, we gain an immediate 'aerial view' of our journey in life, a road-map of our individual life path. Palmistry can zoom in on the important aspects of this journey, make us aware of alternative routes and prepare us for the exciting road ahead.

The Structure of *Palmistry 4 Today*

Palmistry 4 Today aims to introduce the basics of hand analysis in the simplest and most stimulating way possible in order that you can bring your own life experience, observations and personality to the subject. I hope that you will finish reading this book feeling confident that you can look at palms (and palm prints) and be able to make accurate assessments as well as begin to time events.

- **Part 1** demonstrates how much vital information can be read from simple, common sense observations. Here you'll learn to grasp the essentials of hand analysis.
- **Part 2** introduces timing techniques to get you acquainted early on with learning to time and forecast events accurately.
- **Part 3** provides an overview of how palmistry can help with specific areas of life.
- **Part 4** offers an opportunity to test your new skills on a selection of prints. I've presented a handful of profiles including two quizzes to keep you on your toes.

In these four parts, we examine the four essentials of hand analysis (palm lines, hand shape, fingers and skin-ridge patterns) and the four main priorities (love, work, health and timing). Along the way you'll also find the following:

- **Information Boxes** – introducing interesting facts about hand-reading and related research.
- **Synthesis Boxes** – explaining how to bring together the different elements shown in the hand.
- **Hot Tips** – useful tips on various aspects of reading the hand.
- **Print Focus** – revealing the information you can glean only from reading a palm print.

- **Noted Palms** – observations of markings found on the hands of famous, infamous and noteworthy people in the limelight – who have not been clients – along with brief biographical information.

- **Palm Profiles** – analyses of palms, showing how to apply the knowledge given in this book.

- **Quizzes** – to help you test your knowledge.

Frequently Asked Questions

Before moving on to Part 1, I'd like to tackle some of the most common questions palmists are asked.

Do lines on the hand change?

Lines change over time. Some lines appear or disappear in a matter of months, others change slowly over the years, whilst the colour of the Health Line (see page 158) can be a daily indicator of our constitution.

Line changes can reflect new developments in attitude, health or lifestyle. Research has revealed direct links between the nervous system and our palm patterns. For instance, the shape of the Heart Line (which represents emotional attitudes) develops when a child enters puberty, and palm lines fade during the period of an emotional breakdown or during the advance of senility (the fading of the mental faculties). Shocks and changes to lifestyle and body will be reflected in the hand (and even in the fingernails). Taking palm prints over a period of time can prove invaluable in tracking and understanding these developments.

As for the finger prints and dermal patterns, they never change. Even when the hands are injured, once they recover from injury and scar tissue heals, the original patterns return. However, the dermal patterns can be affected if our immune system is weakened. For example, 'stress' lines across the finger tips can appear over the prints.

Is everything already 'written' in the palm?

Our hands show our current state and the direction in which we are taking ourselves. This direction is neither unalterable nor inevitable.

As with the study of astrology, in palmistry we must take into consideration the effects of gender, genetics, education, race, sexuality and the location in which we're born. According to astrologer Jenni Harte, our horoscope represents the 'contract' we make when we are born. In the same way, I think the palm is a manifestation of that contract. I believe that initially we choose the major conditions, opportunities and challenges we experience (our 'contract') as well as a palette of 'tools' (including our character) to assist us. Then we create our life with these, adding different colours, strokes and interpretative flair.

Our hands show this basic 'contract', and they also show the effects of the decisions that we make during the course of our life.

Can anyone learn to read hands?

Absolutely. But although anyone can learn to read hands, we will not all do this in exactly the same way. After teaching seminars on the subject, it became clear to me that some students would make very good 'technical' palmists and concern themselves with the minutiae in the palm, whilst others would read instinctively and capture the general 'feeling' of the hand and its owner. You'll discover your own method along the way. And I've included some tips in Appendix 2 that I think may be useful for anyone wishing to read other people's hands professionally.

I'm often asked if palmists need to be psychic. Intuition certainly helps at times but it's not an essential part of hand analysis. In fact, I always suggest working strictly with the basics of interpretation before venturing into intuitive readings – in this way your understanding of the subject will support you if the intuition fails. You'll find, however, that intuition – along with a greater understanding and acceptance of human nature – develops as you read more hands.

As soon as you tell others of your new interest in palmistry I can guarantee they'll place their hands under your nose for inspection. While astrologers can avoid being challenged on the spot by explaining the complexity of erecting a birth chart and the generalities of sun sign columns, we don't have that luxury. Some of my original students were expected to 'tell fortunes' when they arrived home from their first class! Most people, of course, will want to know just about everything about themselves, and expect you to know when children and money will enter their lives. You may not be able to tell them everything they want to know, but if you can provide a few spot-on observations, it should satisfy the majority and will also begin to build your confidence in your ability to read hands.

In this book we'll be learning the secrets of the palm in a direct, hands-on way. Don't be discouraged by how much there is to learn. Look at the parts that interest you first, then pursue the more challenging or complex areas when you're ready. When I first started to teach this subject I was fascinated by the different methods my students employed to learn – and they were learning the full A to Z, line-by-line syllabus without this book! Some preferred to learn the numerous complexities of the subject, carefully dissecting the direction and meanings of each minor line; others managed to grasp the essence of a palm from their first impressions. This book will teach you both methods, but in the section 'Palm Detective' you will discover that it's important to learn how to get to the 'heart' of the palm. You'll do this best by examining the hand as a whole, rather than getting lost in the minutiae. It's vital to get a 'feel' for the hands in front of you.

Which hand do you read?

Like most palmists, I read both hands. Each hand reveals a particular side of our character – however you wish to refer to them: as masculine and feminine, active and passive, conscious and unconscious. Each hand has an alliance with certain brain functions and each represents a part of our life *regardless of whether we are left- or right-handed* (see 'The Ruling Hand' below).

Contrary to some traditional books on the subject, I don't believe that the left hand alone reveals the past whilst we can glimpse the future only by examining the right hand. Both reflect past, present and future conditions, but it is vital to understand the differences between them before we begin reading hands.

THE LEFT HAND REVEALS:	THE RIGHT HAND REVEALS:
• Our inner self, resources, drives and tensions; our current psychological state; our personal life	• Our public self and drives; how we interact with the outside world and in relationships with others
• The reflective side of our character; our private self and inner psychology	• The side of our character we show others
• Innate abilities; aspirations; potential and our inherited predisposition and talents	• Abilities and talents demonstrated to the outside world; our potential currently being actively developed in the outside world
• The subconscious self	• The conscious self
• Deeper-seated emotions and views of life and love based upon our experience	• Current views of life and love based upon our experiences
It registers the events that affect us psychologically.	It registers the events that affect how we continue to function in the outer world.

Left hand = private/psychological/passive side
Right hand = relationship/public/active side

New markings on the left hand record our emotional and psychological reactions – even if the actual events are not of a personal nature.

New markings on the right hand record tangible changes in any area of life – those that are a direct result of our relationships and interactions.

For example, a new job may require that we speak in public, the thought of which may terrify us. If we have the courage to take on the new role, the building of confidence necessary to perform will be shown in the left hand, whilst the right hand will record the job change and any kudos it brings.

So, in an important way, the left hand is who we truly are – not just the public mask we wish to show others. Character traits in the left hand will be demonstrated most vividly with those we trust, live with or have grown up with. When we fall deeply in love the strengths, insecurities, hopes and psychological issues we so often hide are revealed through this intimate partnership. Our left hand provides an instant 'inside track' to these. Along with the thumbs, index fingers, finger prints and Head Lines, the left hand reveals our true self.

Many palmists reverse the above attributions if the subject is left-handed, that is, the left-hander's left hand will reveal his public/active side, whilst the right will indicate the psychological drives and passive side. After many years of testing differences in left-handers, I have kept to the assignations above *regardless of which hand we use to write*. I believe that we should stick to the original divisions above but suggest that you keep an open mind and investigate further when reading palms for left-handers. Examine both hands to see whether differences in markings can be attributed to a difference between the person's reactions to an event in a more deep-rooted manner or quite literally in their everyday lives.

The Ruling Hand

While we should read both hands it is important to be aware that we all have a ruling hand, one that reveals our innate type of thinking and correlates to our dominant brain hemisphere. Do we have a scientific, orderly mentality? Or are we fluid, imaginative thinkers? Whichever it is, it will be reflected in the hands. In assessing which type of thinking describes you best, please remember that:

- The left hand is more linked to intuition, emotion, memory, music, imagination and the creative urge. It is largely controlled by the right hemisphere of the brain.

- The right hand is more linked to language, science, business, calculation and the rational. It is largely controlled by the left hemisphere of the brain.

Determining your ruling hand

In order to determine which hand (which type of thinking) best describes you, try out the following test, as recommended by hand analyst Peter West.

Interweave your fingers and thumbs. When the left thumb comes out on top, the left hand is dominant – revealing (regardless of whether your are left- or right-handed) a creative, instinctive nature. When the right thumb comes out on top the right hand is dominant – revealing a rational, orderly mentality. I consider this method is perhaps the best way of determining the ruling hand.

As a student palmist I was taught another method: measuring the width of the palms. If the left is the larger of the two, then intuition and instinct dominate your actions. If the right hand is larger than the left, then language and reason predominate.

There's another method proposed by hand analyst Ed Campbell. He suggests we place our hands palm-down on a flat surface. The dominant hand is the one with the closest angle between the index finger and the thumb.

How to read both hands

Examine the left hand first, then compare it with the right hand, noting the differences in palm shape, finger length and the relative positions and lengths of the fingers. Then examine the differences in the lines with care. The left hand represents who we really are – our basic nature, regardless of accomplishments and what we wish to project to the outside world. The right hand is what we want others to see and how we operate professionally and as a member of society.

For example, if the Head Line (how we apply ourselves to tasks and how our mind works) on the right hand is clear and strong yet is weakly formed on the left hand, we can deal successfully with others professionally or socially (right hand) but we take problems very much to heart and are more sensitive and vulnerable on an intimate and psychological level (left hand).

Another example: if the Fate Line (our direction and life path) is broken (indicating a change or disruption) on the left hand but not on the right, the change affects us on a personal level (left hand) without disrupting the way we function in the outer world (right hand). If this break is on the right hand but not the left, we continue our personal path uninterrupted by a physical move or job shift (right hand).

In many hands there are only a few differences that jump out immediately. In the example given in Palm Print 2, we can observe that both hands look quite similar in appearance. The most noticeable difference occurs on this man's Fate Line (the strong line running up the centre of the palm towards the middle finger). While the left hand's Fate Line branches in two and has a short line

Palm Print 2
Comparing left and right hands

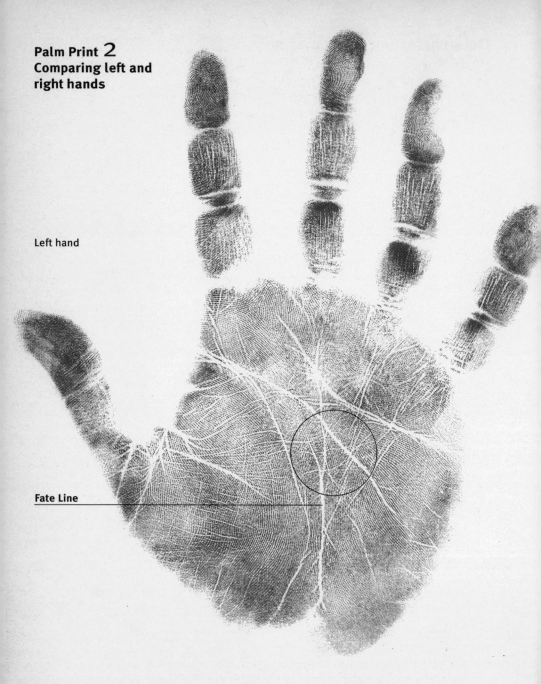

Left hand

Fate Line

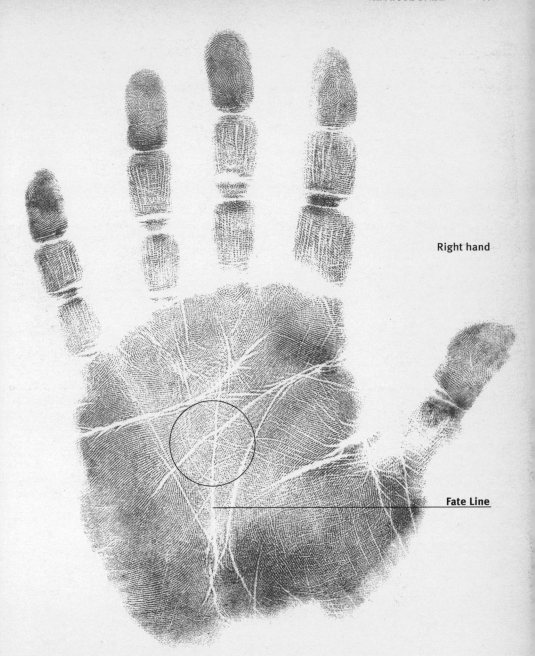

Right hand

Fate Line

reaching up to join it, the right hand's Fate Line continues steadily up the palm. Later we'll discover more about these Influence Lines that join the Fate Line (see pages 137–8) – these signify important people who enter our life and shape its path (as represented by the Fate Line).

This man began a personal relationship at the age of 32 that improved his psychological attitude (left hand) towards trusting others, helping him to discover himself through this partnership. The mutually supportive relationship also gave him greater confidence to pursue his own personal goals (the Fate Line splits, with one branch heading towards the index finger, a sign of greater self-direction and self-realisation). He continued his attitude to his work routine and responsibilities without interruption (the unbroken Fate Line on the right hand).

Taking Palm Prints

After reading this book, you'll never look at hands the same way again. You will have learned how the hands reveal character, and emotional, sexual and health matters – and that even the ways we hold our palms and fingers reveal character traits. So before you go any further, make an ink print of both your palms. (See Appendix 1 for instructions.) It's important to learn to take prints because there's so much extra information about us that can only be seen this way.

By studying the palm prints in this book you'll discover that it's not always easy to take clear palm prints. Some people's palms were difficult to print, often because of the hollow centre of their palms. Others were done in haste because the individual was extremely busy. These experiences serve to remind us that we should practise printing and, where possible, take additional prints until we're satisfied.

Although *Palmistry 4 Today* is packed with palm prints, you can learn most facets of the subject without ever taking prints. In fact, you'll need to study real hands to accumulate experience, as well as observe skin texture, colour, nails and the fine line details that prints occasionally obscure. Learn to look at both prints and real hands, and expand your knowledge by studying both the hands and the hand prints of friends and family. This will increase your confidence in dealing with future clients, as well as helping you to understand yourself and your loved ones. And whilst you're doing all of this, you'll find a method of reading palms that's unique to you.

Note: The prints presented in this book are mostly of right hands, but they have been reversed to make it easier to relate to when looking directly at your own hands.

PART 1

PALM DETECTIVE

First Impressions

You can learn the basics of palmistry quickly enough to begin making valuable observations almost immediately. Although it may be daunting to consider absorbing the volume of information there is on the palm, you can gather key components of the subject by learning to trust your gut instincts from your first impressions of someone's hands.

A Busy or Empty Palm?

Let's jump in at the deep end. The following questions will demonstrate how easy it is to get an accurate first impression of the hands. Let's begin playing Palm Detective.

> **Q: From your overall impression of the two palms in Palm Print 3, who do you think is more highly-strung and nervous: Palm A or B?**

Look at the numerous, fine lines on Palm B. What does this suggest to you? To me this palm looks more sensitive, impressionable and susceptible than Palm A. The delicate web of lines all over Palm B suggests that this person would appear highly-strung and nervous. Their emotional make-up would be more complicated than that suggested by Palm A, which has fewer lines. Palm A looks 'simpler', and we can deduce that the person is more straightforward emotionally in their approach to life, and less prone to worry or tension. The more lines on the hand, the higher the emotional receptivity and reaction to external events.

Palm Print 3
Busy and empty palms

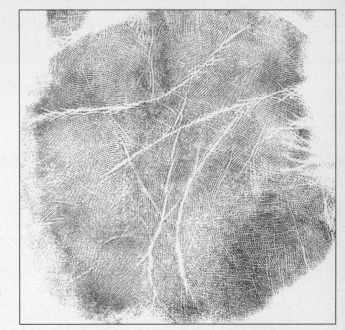

Palm A: Hand print of a successful industrialist who quit his work at the age of 33 to focus on creative ventures

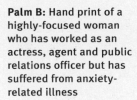

Palm B: Hand print of a highly-focused woman who has worked as an actress, agent and public relations officer but has suffered from anxiety-related illness

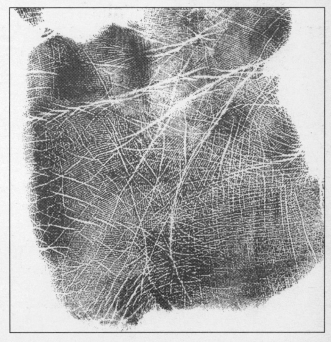

MANY FINE, SPIDERY LINES ON THE PALM SHOW:

- A greater sensitivity to hurt and criticism

- Nervous tension and nervous (emotional) energy

- An ability to pick up feelings of discord (can sense atmospheres expertly)

- A vulnerability to negative people

- An up-and-down roller-coaster of emotions; hypersensitivity

- A tendency towards psychosomatic illness

- A need for (as well as anticipation of and involvement in) emotional crises and drama

With 'busy' hands we need to relax, take time off and avoid people who swamp us with emotional or practical problems. Remaining stress-free keeps us physically balanced and mentally healthy.

FEW LINES ON THE PALM SHOW:

- Little emotional complexity or worry

- A need for, and enjoyment of, life's basic physical comforts: food, drink and regular sex

- A tough 'I can cope' exterior often masking hidden worries

- A practical sensibility, but often accompanied by black-or-white judgements

- A dislike of delving into deeper emotions

- Greater physical robustness

- Stress from blocking out emotional situations for long periods

With 'empty' hands we need to understand the sensitivity of others and get in touch with our own inner emotional needs. Having the courage to express our feelings will help us relate to others more effectively.

Although the hand does react over time to a great deal of physical activity and the lines can be strengthened by manual work or exercise, it is interesting to note that the general folding of the hands from use does not create the numerous fine lines we would expect to see. Nor does folding explain the many differences found between palms. In fact, manual workers are more likely to have few lines on their hands, while the nervous worrier who neither works nor exercises will often have a web of fine lines over his or her palms. In addition, hand analyst Lori Reid states that full hands (numerous lines) are more resilient and able to withstand greater pain than empty hands (few lines). She says that those who have fewer lines rely on short, sharp bursts of energy and can have their vitality drained easily.

Palm Print 4
Bold and fragile lines

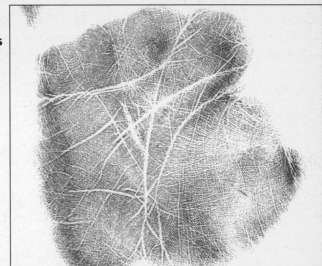

Palm A: Hand print of an outwardly confident young man who now runs the family business

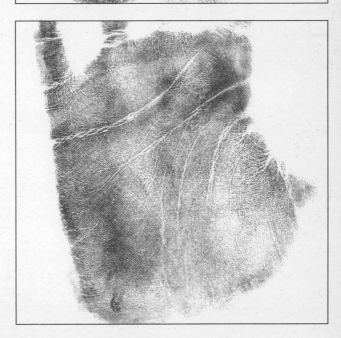

Palm B: Hand print of a clever businesswoman (see page 132)

Q: From your overall impression of the two palms in Palm Print 4, who do you think has more purpose, clarity of thought and action, Palm A or B?

Look at the boldness of the lines on Palm A. This reveals purpose and a determination to experience life to the full, whereas on Palm B the lines appear fragile and lacking in energy and get-up-and-go.

STRONG, CLEAR LINES REVEAL:

- Ambition, drive and self-motivation
- A self-determining and energetic response to life
- Direction and a healthy measure of self-belief

We need to continue to live life in the present, to enjoy the challenges, obstacles and triumphs. We should aim for balance in our lifestyle: paying equal attention to our physical, professional, emotional and relational well-being.

WEAK OR FEATHERY LINES REVEAL A CURRENT:

- Lack of involvement in everyday life
- Half-hearted, lethargic attitude to situations
- Fear of failure
- Problem with the physical constitution
- Incorrect choice of diet or a lack of exercise
- State of negativity, indecision or lack of direction

To strengthen our lines we need to develop more fighting spirit and have the courage to live each day to the fullest. We should become more sociable, avoid wasting opportunities to enjoy life and be careful not to wallow in self-pity or cling on to problems in the past.

Occasionally we may come across a person with very deeply etched lines, which are less visible on prints. This indicates that they may have extreme reactions to life and should protect themselves from those who prey on vulnerable people and exploit others' weaknesses to cover their own. With these deep, thick (often very red) lines, they experience life in the raw. Past hurts have probably been ingrained deeply on the psyche. There is an over-sensitivity and a sense of drama, and they unwittingly attract crisis. I call this the 'nails down a blackboard' approach to life. Their intensity and vulnerability is often hard to hide. These people can best express their pain by sharing their thoughts on past experiences with others.

Grasping the Essence of the Hand

When trying to grasp the essence of the hand it is important to remember that the individual markings on a palm are relative to the character and motivations of the individual, as well as to their age and the crossroads they are at in their life. In this book, we will learn to recognise the prime motivations of a person – whether, for example, they are driven by financial or emotional security. A person who is materialistic may consider losing their job a far greater trauma than the loss of a partner. A widow may experience her husband's death as a new beginning to her life. In both cases *their hands will reveal their reactions rather than the actual event.* For example, for some people Ambition Lines (see page 187) will indicate the birth of a child, while for others these lines will indicate a new business or a new life away from home restrictions. The key to understanding markings on a hand lies in examining the client's basic character, as seen in the shape of the hand, finger print patterns and dominant lines on the palm. In short, markings are determined by the ways in which we respond to that particular occurrence: a difficulty can only be experienced as such if we respond in that manner.

By understanding fundamental points such as what is this person really like, what talents do they have, how do they react to challenges and what motivates them, you will be able to understand yourself and others better. For those of you who want to take the areas covered in this book one step further and look at palmistry as a future profession, check out the advice in Appendix 2.

The 4-Step Guide to Becoming a Palm Detective

When you understand the fundamentals of palmistry, you'll be on your way to making accurate assessments. When reading palms you'll first need to accumulate information from the following, as shown in Palm Print 5, and described in the following sections:

1. The size and shape of the hand
2. The major palm lines
3. The fingers and thumb
4. Finger print patterns

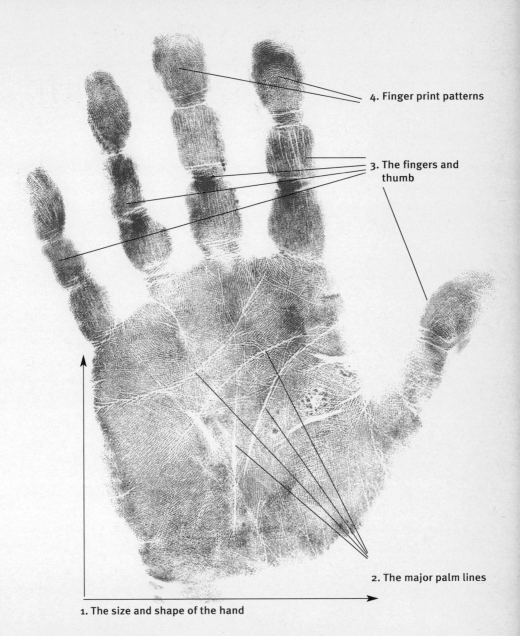

4. Finger print patterns

3. The fingers and
   thumb

2. The major palm lines

1. The size and shape of the hand

Palm Print 5
The 4-step guide to becoming a palm detective

Step 1
The Size and Shape of the Hand

Our Personal Approach and Basic Motivations

The size and the shape of our hands reflects our fundamental approach to life and our basic drives. In this section we will consider large and small hands, square and rectangular palms, long and short fingers, the relationship between hand shape and the four elements, and the palm mounts.

Large, Small or Average Hands?

Judging our hand size *in proportion to the rest of our body* will provide the first important assessment of character from our hands. Although we must take into account our height and size, a simple method to estimate the hand size is to compare it to the length of the face. An average hand should extend from the chin to the middle of the forehead (so long as we avoid folding our palm to accommodate our nose!).

The proportional size of the hand provides us with information about *our style, method, technique and personal approach to work and tasks*. In most cases our hands reflect our general build and fall into the 'average' size category, and therefore the information in the following two sections may not apply to you personally, but it could be of great advantage when dealing with co-workers, employees, loved ones and colleagues. For example, recognising that someone has small or large hands can eliminate the perennial problem at work of placing round pegs into square holes. Use this section to gain an understanding of where a person's basic organisational talents lie and the areas of life to which they are best suited.

Large hands

We might expect people with large hands to take on large projects and have a general air of authority, controlling their environment, but perhaps to be quite physically clumsy with their hands. Well, contrary to expectation, large hands are found on those of us who possess greater manual dexterity than our small-handed counterparts. We enjoy smaller tasks and excel in detailed work, and if our fingers happen to be longer than average too, we may also have a fastidiousness to our nature. In general, we have smaller handwriting and can be precise, being able to concentrate on the minutiae of detail. We are the perfectionists who can work endlessly on projects the rest of the world would have put in the cupboard months ago. Jigsaws, intricate sewing and figurine painting are just three examples of tasks that require the intricacy, dedication and concentration that appeal to us.

Interestingly, we tend not to be the ones in positions of leadership. This is often due to a lack of interest in the overall, bigger picture. Most of us would feel lost organising large-scale activities and projects, and are better suited to the smaller tasks and manual work that provide the foundation of business and industry. With large hands we would rather not make the big decisions, take the leaps of faith required or have to juggle numerous tasks simultaneously. At times we would benefit from seeing the whole picture, as this would give us greater security in planning our lives and work. The key to our personal success and happiness is focus, planning, detailed precision and a love of doing a job well. We can look forward to enjoying our twilight years as times of creativity – finding ways to indulge our favourite pastimes.

In love, we who have large hands can be extra attentive, thoughtful and patient but must avoid putting our over-critical nature to constant use. Others should not be surprised to find that we enjoy spending much time studiously examining them! We are the type to appreciate the little things that make up a strong relationship. As precise perfectionists, we take trouble to get things just right.

Small hands

Those of us with smaller hands are fast workers and usually quick thinkers. We thrive on stimulating environments, deadlines and busy lifestyles where there is an endless set of challenges to meet on a daily basis. We are the ones with the bold, sometimes dramatic or majestic, handwriting that shouts 'Notice me!'

We have the potential to be entrepreneurs and to make money fast, and we are able to make quick decisions. Jumping on board with a new idea (or pioneering one ourselves), we organise the work and then delegate matters that require fine-tuning. We have an impressive ability to handle numerous situations as well as to juggle people, problems and stress successfully. We have a canny knack of sensing the outcome of a project, but need the help of others to do the donkey work. Great supervisors and managers of big projects and large ideas, we often branch out into new fields to conquer more challenging situations and take chances based upon hunches. Although we can sense the overall perspective and see future trends, our weakness is a disregard for detail or the small print. However, most of us would feel lost and, in particular, bored if placed in a job with few opportunities to expand. We lose interest if inundated with red tape, small detail and analysis. We need stimulation to get ahead and move on up the career ladder. If we can't do that we'll happily seek investment from others and build a ladder of our own.

In love, repartee and a meeting of sharp minds are prerequisites for us, and we can leave slower, larger-handed people behind. Impatience is certainly a trait that both benefits and harms us, as is a propensity towards irritability when the world is just too slow for us.

Square or Rectangular Palms?

Measure the width of your palm from the widest point under the little finger to the corner where your thumb meets the palm. Measure the length by starting from under the ring finger to the base of the palm at the wrist. If this second measurement is significantly longer, then your palm is rectangular. If the two measurements are of similar dimensions, then the palm is considered square. This classification and the elemental system that follows are methods of revealing our basic desires, drives and needs.

A square palm indicates that we have a practical nature, while a rectangular palm indicates a more intuitive nature.

The practical (square) palm

The most important characteristics of those of us with square palms are that we feel comfortable dealing with everyday situations and wish to approach life in a practical, productive manner. This practicality may be more of a desire than an actuality (the Head Line will provide clues as to whether we can naturally apply ourselves in a practical way – see pages 52–9). Nevertheless the need for order, routine and consistency is an important personality drive. We often long for change in our environment and to see long-standing situations develop, move on or alter completely. We would love a more exciting life, but it is our basic need, however, to remain in a stable, supporting environment. The drive for financial security, to be the provider and future planner, is what dominates and keeps us generally conservative. It means we are stalwarts, responsible people who can show tremendous loyalty because we are here for 'the long stay'. On both a personal and professional level, we would see better results if we became more adaptable.

Palm Print 6
The square palm

The square palm of a
female debt-collector

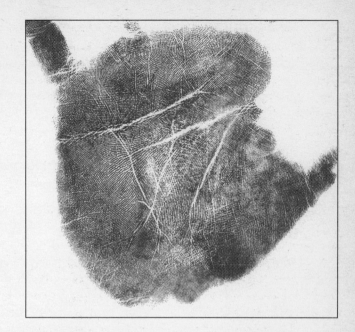

Palm Print 7
The rectangular palm

The rectangular palm of
a restless, sensitive man
working in the media

The intuitive (rectangular) palm

Whereas the prime motivations of the square palm are for order, productivity and constancy in everyday life, we who have rectangular palms aim to have a life of less responsibility – fewer of the everyday situations that can tire, bore or tie us down. We rely on intuition to make decisions and would rather avoid the nitty-gritty of facts and figures. Those with square palms look at facts and past performance and assess these before making judgements. With rectangular palms we make better choices by relying on instinct – what *feels* right to us. We have hunches and can be unusually receptive to the emotions of others. This makes us sympathetic friends and partners, but we need to avoid being unreliable, changeable or too selfish. We tend to be more artistic than people with square palms (a straight Head Line would indicate an instinct to market our talents successfully; a curved Head Line could indicate that we indulge in creative pursuits without practically pursuing financial reward for our artistic hobbies). Others should not expect us to come to their defence in a practical way, as we prefer to avoid the rough edges of life; we do not like to deal with unpleas-antness or aggression. We can be inspiring, creative people who see the potential in others and the beauty in life, but without some grounding or accountability for our actions we risk having a recklessly rose-tinted view of life.

Long or Short Fingers?

Open your hand and look at the palm (rather than the back of the hand). Measure the middle finger. If it is roughly 7/8ths of the length of the palm or greater, you can conclude that your fingers are long. Occasionally the middle finger will look short compared to the fingers on either side. When this is the case, this finger should be at least 6/8ths of the length of the palm for all the fingers to be classified as long.

Finger length adds to the information we can acquire from studying the Head Line, which we shall discover more about later. The Head Line reveals how we think and develop ideas; the length of our fingers – in relation to the palm – reveals the manner in which we approach and evaluate this information. Both the Head Line and finger length determine the extent of our mental dexterity, but it is as though the fingers are the instruments that play and interpret the notes composed by the Head Line.

Long fingers

We are highly sensitive and in tune with atmospheres. Although careful with our words, we can be quite emotionally insensitive to the feelings of others when in a relationship. We always seem to be finding fault, too, and our pickiness can drive others to distraction. In relationships we often have high standards, particularly in matters of personal hygiene. We are thinkers and planners who love to analyse details; we make good researchers and tacticians. We long to have our world in order and can spend long periods making lists of lists to help us when we finally tackle a problem. Checking out our home or work desk is a good way of understanding our mental equilibrium at any current moment in our life! Others sometimes see us as exasperatingly slow and fussy, but we are resourceful and competent because we are thorough and critical.

Long fingers and palm shape

- Square palms with long fingers belong to reliable people who can plan ahead but need to avoid being too ruled by routine to enjoy life's adventures.

- Rectangular palms with long fingers are the dreamers who must find ways of converting these aspirations into tangible results.

Short fingers

We hate having to read the entire instruction manual! We want to grasp the essence, tackle the matter quickly and move on. We just haven't the patience to sit down and learn page by page. We can be somewhat rough and ready, slightly slap-dash and often merrily overlook the finer points. Jumping to conclusions we can miss the subtleties, but are good at clearing up urgent problems or tearing

SYNTHESIS PART 1: FINGER LENGTH AND THE HEAD LINE

Look for balance in the hand by examining the Head Line (see pages 52–9). Long fingers should ideally be on a hand with a long Head Line, and short fingers should accompany a short Head Line. When they correlate, there's a natural balance in the thought process and a natural progression from thought into action – similar to when a musical piece is played by an instrument for which it was naturally written. Often a lack of balance will show a propensity towards neurosis, insecurity or uncertainty. Very often these extreme traits can propel people to successful lives – but at what cost? The key is to make the most out of any imbalance and to watch out for extreme reactions or self-destructive behaviour as, for example, in playing the self-saboteur.

through red tape, because we are able to grasp the nub of the problem and get to the heart of the matter. We should leave the small print on that essential contract to others. Very short fingers reveal bluntness and a forthright quality that can upset the diplomatic long-fingered person. Some may even sniff that we lack social graces as we bulldoze our way through life.

Short fingers and palm shape

- Square palms with short fingers are practical people who aim to build a secure foundation for themselves, but they should not lose sight of their emotional needs.

- Rectangular palms with short fingers are quick to begin new projects and affairs but need solid foundations to support their efforts.

The Four Elements: Fire, Earth, Air and Water

In recent years many palmists have adopted a four-fold system devised in the 1960s by palmist Fred Gettings that correlates to the four elements: Fire, Earth, Air and Water. Some palmists have added a final, fifth type – the Mixed hand – for those hybrid hands that don't fit neatly into one group or another.

The shape of the hand – its particular element – gives us strong indications as to what motivates us. It is first chapter of our life story – the introduction that unravels our basic temperament and emotional needs. By recognising the basic shape (element) of a hand we can then seek to understand the essence of the person. Are they driven by financial reward? Do emotional needs or intellectual ones motivate them?

Many student palmists have trouble assessing this aspect of hand analysis as, unfortunately for us, most hands are not pure elemental types, making classification tricky. Knowing your zodiac sign's element (for example, Aquarius is an Air sign) is not a reliable indicator of your palm's elemental shape either. Earth-shaped hands, for example, sometimes contain fine, watery-looking lines. I would suggest that while gaining an understanding of the hand shape can provide clear insights into basic character motivations, it is wise not to get caught up with trying to fit everything neatly into a category. Understanding the four elements as key personality types will be a good foundation for understanding character, but it is important not to rely too heavily on any one aspect of palmistry alone.

Diagram 1:
The Fire hand

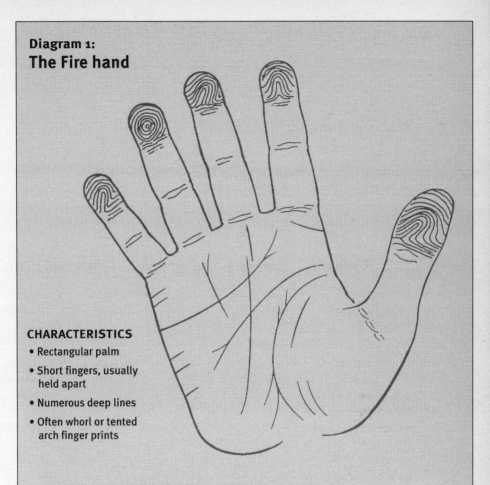

CHARACTERISTICS

- Rectangular palm
- Short fingers, usually held apart
- Numerous deep lines
- Often whorl or tented arch finger prints

PERSONALITY MOTIVATIONS AND CHARACTERISTICS IN RELATIONSHIPS AND WORK

- Adventurous, passionate, spontaneous, enthusiastic, impulsive, audacious
- Self-interested and self-motivated
- Seek active, exciting lives with challenge, deadlines and risk; have a low boredom threshold and hate routine
- Self-promoters, Svengalis, hustlers, agents, pioneers, show-offs and entertainers
- Inspire others to follow and can achieve greater recognition than can peers; political animals who put on a display of bravado; often leave matters to the last moment
- Need reassurance from the physical act of love
- Quick to anger but quick to forgive

Diagram 2:
The Earth hand

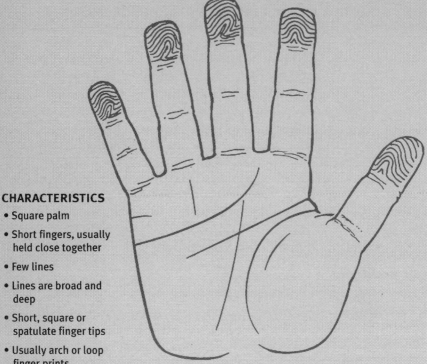

CHARACTERISTICS

- Square palm
- Short fingers, usually held close together
- Few lines
- Lines are broad and deep
- Short, square or spatulate finger tips
- Usually arch or loop finger prints
- Clear skin ridge patterns

PERSONALITY MOTIVATIONS AND CHARACTERISTICS IN RELATIONSHIPS AND WORK

- Practical, conservative, reliable, steady, productive, private
- Motivated by security, expediency, tangible results and taking care of business
- Seek regularity in routine, income and deadlines

- Builders, craftsmen, businessmen, gardeners, farmers, country-lovers, cooks, sportsmen
- Stable, supportive workers who derive pleasure from building, developing and a job done well
- Need warm-hearted partners with whom to express themselves physically

Diagram 3:
The Air hand

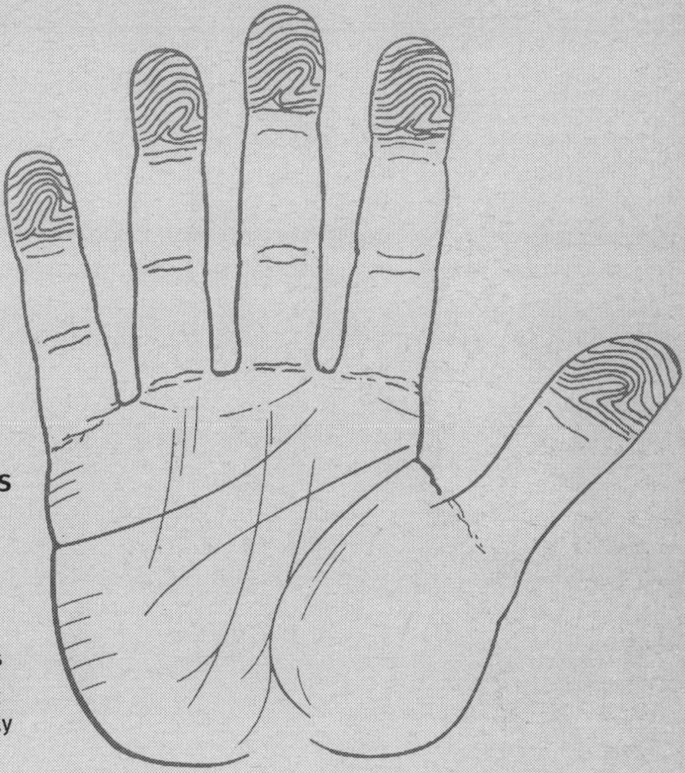

CHARACTERISTICS

- Square palm
- Long fingers
- Strong clear lines
- Spatulate or rounded finger tips
- Various finger print patterns but usually loop or loop-arch
- Sometimes a Creative Curve (see page 82)

PERSONALITY MOTIVATIONS AND CHARACTERISTICS IN RELATIONSHIPS AND WORK

- Expressive, curious, witty, sociable, questioning, bon vivant, versatile, highly-strung
- Motivated by concepts, ideas, exchange, debate and learning new things rather than by financial reward
- Seek stimulating lives with variety, travel and regular change
- Communicators of all kinds: internet, telephone, media
- Need to work with others, exchanging ideas
- Look for intelligent partners who never tire of travel and conversation

Diagram 4:
The Water hand

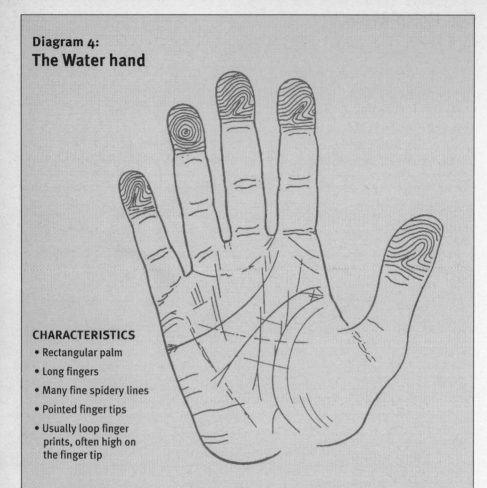

CHARACTERISTICS

- Rectangular palm
- Long fingers
- Many fine spidery lines
- Pointed finger tips
- Usually loop finger prints, often high on the finger tip

PERSONALITY MOTIVATIONS AND CHARACTERISTICS IN RELATIONSHIPS AND WORK

- Sensitive, artistic, emotional, receptive, caring, impressionable, moody
- Unmotivated by ego, seek an emotional response from others
- Look for harmony, contentment and peace but often experience dramatic situations and crises; lives are impacted by life and death issues

- Counsellors, therapists, carers and other careers involving perception and public awareness; should avoid competitive environments
- Need, in some way at work, to be of service and help the human condition
- Seek emotionally tender partners who are tied to tradition or the home

The Palm Mounts

Under each finger and across the palm are raised areas of flesh known as mounts. Although the mounts are featured heavily in older palmistry books, I haven't found the size or position of these to be particularly important in hand analysis. However, the mounts under each of the four fingers do share the attributes of those fingers (as listed on page 73), so this is important when assessing the effects of a line beginning or ending on a mount. For example, a Head Line (mentality and reasoning) that begins under the index finger will reflect an authoritative, ambitious mind and a powerfully persuasive person, confident of their ideas and usually in possession of high ideals.

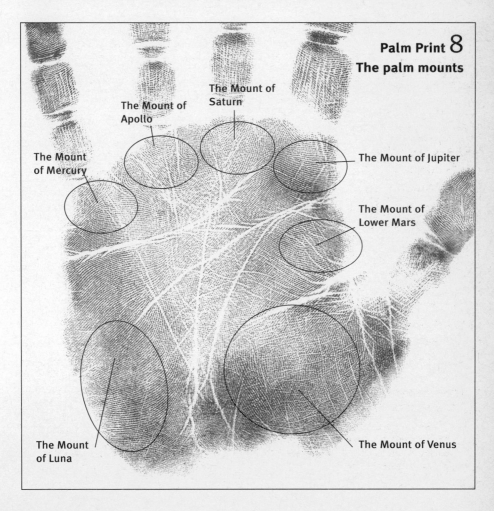

Palm Print 8
The palm mounts

The Mount of Saturn

The Mount of Apollo

The Mount of Jupiter

The Mount of Mercury

The Mount of Lower Mars

The Mount of Luna

The Mount of Venus

The three mounts to be aware of with regard to character are the Mount of Luna (the Moon), the Mount of Lower Mars and the Mount of Venus. On the Mount of Luna we also find the Travel Lines (see page 187) and the Matriarch Line (see page 155). On the Mount of Venus we may also find the Mars Line (see page 170) as well as any Friendship Lines (see page 140).

The Mount of Luna

Here lies the realm of the imagination, memory of the past, psychic intuition and mysterious fantasy worlds. According to palmist Lori Reid, the Mount of Luna governs 'our subconscious impressions and unconscious drives, instincts and imagination'. When the mount is large, our creative instinct is powerful, as is our sensitivity and receptivity. When it is pink, we can encounter more than our fair share of intuitive experiences and have the opportunity to venture into the exploration of psychic phenomena. A raised Mount of Luna or a curved Head Line diving into this mount will colour our personality with the following traits: imagination, mysticism, impressionability, susceptibility and escapism.

The Mount of Lower Mars

When fleshy, the Mount of Lower Mars indicates a provocative person who is challenging both verbally and physically.

The Mount of Venus

The Mount of Venus shows the extent of our physical warmth in a relationship. Raise the wrist and turn the palm to 90° to see how prominent it is and how far it extends into the palm. When this mount is padded, pronounced or protruding into the palm, we express warmth and vitality, and a strong appetite for life (as well as for food, sex and drink). When it is dominant, we give large helpings of love and sympathy and ask for equal measure in return. Redness of this area will add to our passion. The Mount of Venus also puffs up when we are in the first bloom of romance. When this mount is narrow (seen by a Life Line that does not extend fully into the hand) or flat, we need to develop more energy and warmth in our lives, rather than simply looking for others to provide these for us. A raised Mount of Venus or a mount extending into the palm (at least as far as underneath the centre of the middle finger) will dominate our personality, adding the following characteristics to our psychological make-up: joie de vivre, passion, sensuality, over-indulgence.

QUICK QUIZ 1

1. Which group prefers to spend time working on detailed, precise jobs – large- or small-handed people?

2. With a rectangular palm do we make better choices when we rely on intuition or hard facts?

3. Which type is more likely to be critical – those with long or short fingers?

4. Which element is motivated by a need for material stability?

5. Which element is best suited to media work?

(Answers in Appendix 3, page 218.)

Step 2
The Major Palm Lines

Charting Our Personality

The major lines of the palm are shown in Palm Print 9. Each of these major lines represents a particular kind of energy, an area of life and a type of personality.

Line	Energy	Represents	Personality Type
The Life Line	Fire	Physical constitution and energy	Involvement in life
The Head Line	Air	Thought processes	Decision-making abilities and reasoning
The Heart Line	Water	Emotional make-up	Capacity for affection
The Fate Line	Earth	Life path and direction	Duties, responsibilities and work regime

A helpful way to remember the theme of each line is to associate its meaning with one of the four elements as described earlier. The associations I use are shown in the Table above and are different from those used by other palmists. I see the Life Line's measure of joie de vivre, energy and passion for life as being similar to the element of Fire. The Head Line tells of our ability to communicate and make decisions, and corresponds well to the rationality of Air. The Heart Line's emotionality mirrors the element of Water. Finally, the Fate Line correlates strongly to Earth and this element's work ethic, desire for responsibility and routine.

Occasionally you'll notice that people have one line that crosses the palm instead of the Head and Heart Lines. This is known as the Simian Line. We'll meet this fascinating sign of intensity on page 66. It could best be described as a combination of Air and Water – capable of swamping the intellect with emotion or cooling the sensitivity with hard-line reason.

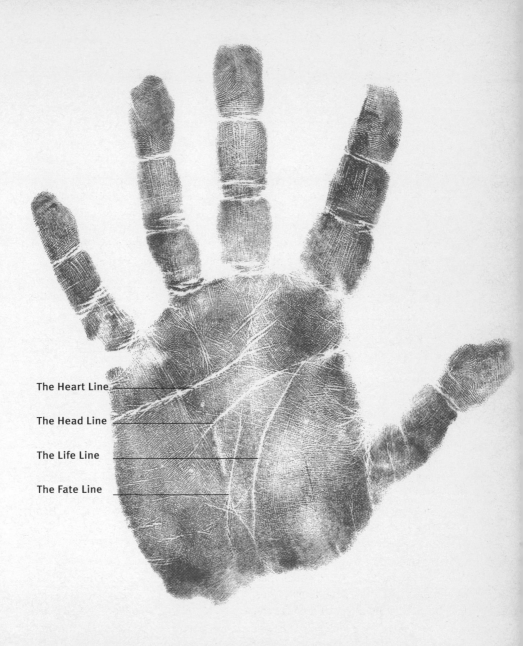

The Heart Line

The Head Line

The Life Line

The Fate Line

Palm Print 9
The major lines of the palm

The Key to Understanding Lines

The major lines on our palms represent our physical, mental, emotional and sexual energies. Their course, colour and depth should be examined, as well as their absence or any interruptions to the line. See the lines as journeys from A to Z. This will help to unravel the story told in each line. Note where the line originates and where it is heading. If we understand the routes of the major lines, where they branch off, and where they fade or strengthen, we'll get a clear idea about their importance, effect and meaning.

From the palm print (or a close examination of the hand) identify the strongest line (the most prominent by length or depth on the print or as seen by the eye). This indicates where most of our energy and thought is currently directed.

- A strong Heart Line reveals a hotbed of emotions and warns of relation-ships or sex dominating thoughts and actions.

- A faint Heart Line betrays a current difficulty in expressing affection.

- When the Life Line is dominant there's a need to enjoy life to the full but energy levels may be erratic.

- When the Life Line is faint we lack get-up-and-go.

- With a very conspicuous Head Line there may be excellent results at work because of our exceptional focus and concentration, or there may be stress from attempting to salvage a situation that is beyond rescue.

- When the Head Line is faint, we are using few of our educational or analytical skills at work.

- When the Fate Line is the strongest, we are driven or weighed down by responsibilities such as putting food on the table, or need to work flat-out. This is often at the expense of other parts of our life.

- When the Fate Line is faint, we are not motivated to succeed in the eyes of the world or we avoid routine and obligations.

- As we grow older we can expect the Fate Line to grow lighter in a print of our palms – unless we refuse to slow down or we take on fresh responsibilities of children and grandchildren.

Double lines

The doubling-up of a line or the appearance of two separate lines suggests duality and increases the importance of the line.

- Two Life Lines (not the usually faint, shorter Mars Line, see page 170) increase energy and fighting spirit.

- Two Head Lines suggests great mental dexterity and a strong split between public and private self (see page 197).

Palm Print 10
Two Life Lines

- Two Heart Lines increase the emotional sensitivity.

- Two Fate Lines running along side each other indicate the presence of two areas (or jobs) that demand our energies and provide double responsibilities (such as parenthood and work). Note that this will often only show on the hand if we feel both areas are equally time-consuming or demanding.

The following markings are shown in Diagram 5.

a. **Forks ('v'):** decision time; travelling down a new road; a division of energies; taking advantage of a double talent or life (see page 196).

b. **Overlapping lines:** planned changes in reaction to recent events; a new outlook or way of living (see pages 109–13).

c. **Square box on a line:** difficult times and uneasy transitions, though we will get through them; a feeling of protection during a stressful period of change or greater responsibilities (for example, raising children).

d. **Sudden stop:** a parting of the ways; the ending of a chapter; time for reinvention and starting over (see pages 109-11).

e. **Gaps:** a period of adjustment, time-off or unemployment (see pages 109–10).

f. **Islands:** feelings of isolation or loneliness; feeling trapped in a situation; motivation and energy are low at this time (see pages 119–21).

g. **Dots:** a black cloud over plans; delays and worry.

h. **Sloping lines from the Life Line into the palm:** new adventures and journeys, perhaps abroad; restless and keen to travel or move country.

i. **Rising lines:** making an effort to succeed or to branch out; the longer the line the greater our expectations of success and accomplishment; numerous rising lines (particularly along the path of the Life Line) show ambition, purpose and success (see pages 190 and 192).

j. **Sloping lines (not on the Life Line):** a feeling of loss or despondency; courage is needed to soldier on (see page 167).

k. **Fine crossing lines:** interference and obstacles; setbacks; meeting new people and situations (see pages 122–3).

l. **Stars:** an explosion of energy or interest; a shock to the system (see pages 160 and 173).

Diagram 5:
Important markings often found on the major palm lines

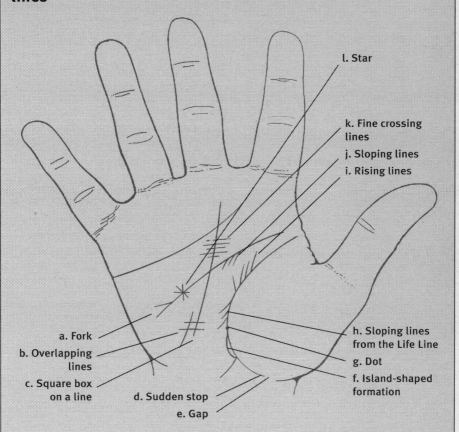

l. Star

k. Fine crossing lines

j. Sloping lines

i. Rising lines

h. Sloping lines from the Life Line

g. Dot

f. Island-shaped formation

a. Fork

b. Overlapping lines

c. Square box on a line

d. Sudden stop

e. Gap

Strong lines: living with purpose, energy and passion in that area of life (i.e. the area 'ruled' by the line in question).

Feathery lines: vulnerability, emotional or physical delicacy, needing to feel more secure in the area concerned.

Woolly lines (on a print): confusion and uncertainty, vagueness, needing clearer direction and focus.

The Life Line: Our Vitality and Energy

The Life Line is often the most dominant line on the hand, wrapping itself around the thumb. At the beginning of 'Palm Detective' we discovered how clear, strong lines in the hand reveal energy and self-determination. The Life Line is the single most important line for assessing our vigour and physical constitution. Its appearance backs up the general robustness or fragility of the rest of the lines on the hand. The answers to questions such as how involved are we in life and what our present state of health is can be revealed by closer examination of this line. It reveals the *quality* rather than the length of our life.

Q: Looking at Palm Print 11, who has the stronger constitution and general better health, Palm A or Palm B?

Palm A's Life Line certainly looks more robust than that of Palm B. A's Life Line appears indomitable, full of energy and vitality. This person enjoys life to the full. The Life Line of Palm B looks delicate and does not move down and into the palm with strength or confidence.

Our Life Line is our own personal autobiography in the palm of our hands, reflecting the decisions and choices we make. Illnesses, periods of restriction, personal accomplishments and obstacles are registered on this line. Research indicates that the Life Line is the first to appear on the hand (from around the top of the thumb, outwards and downwards), by approximately seven weeks of pregnancy.

Check out the section 'Timing Techniques' to time and trace the obstacles you've overcome and the hard-won achievements as you scan your Life Line.

One of the biggest misnomers in hand analysis is the belief that a short Life Line is indicative of a short life and vice versa. Pure nonsense! A short line is more commonly a sign of giving up on situations too soon – of not having the courage or energy to battle on. At times, particularly when seen on the left hand only, there is a feeling of rootlessness, perhaps because in childhood the family never spent too long settled in one area or home.

Palm Print 11 Strong and weak Life Lines

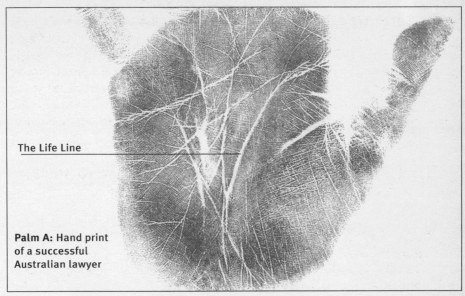

The Life Line

Palm A: Hand print
of a successful
Australian lawyer

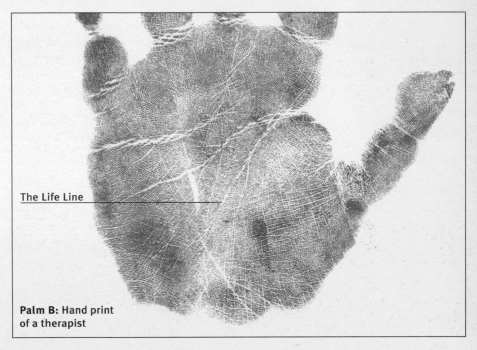

The Life Line

Palm B: Hand print
of a therapist

A STRONG, CLEAR LIFE LINE REVEALS:

- Physical strength and energy
- Resilience and a good immune system
- Clearness about goals and life direction
- Confidence to tackle life head-on

The stronger the line, the more we are able to keep battling and overcoming the obstacles we encounter in life. We never say die and can show great stamina. As with other lines, the clearer and more pronounced the line the more we are involved in life, with people and the circumstances around us.

A WEAK, THIN OR CHAINED LIFE LINE BETRAYS:

- A lack of energy or inability to direct energies constructively
- Weaker recuperative powers
- A lethargic, negative or apathetic approach to life
- A fear of the unknown and of taking risks

If we possess a weak-looking Life Line, we need to develop our physical stamina and become more passionate about our life and projects. A Mars Line (page 170) can help fight off illness and negativity, although if the Mars Line is stronger (as in the hand of Antonia – page 132) it can fuel us with aggression and frustration.

The Head Line: Our Thinking Process

I consider the Head Line, along with the thumb, to be the most significant factor in determining our attitudes and our potential for success in life. If we recognise our aptitudes and particular type of reasoning from our Head Line, we can ascertain our own individual path to fulfilment. Determining the type of Head Line we have will help us – and employers – avoid the perennial problem of placing people in the wrong type of job. Of course, the thumb, hand shape and finger print patterns provide further verification, so we should look at these in depth, too. First, let's take a look at how the shape of the Head Line determines our intellectual viewpoint.

Curved or straight Head Line?

If the Head Line on one hand is straight while on the other hand it is curved this can indicate indecision, an unpredictable nature or someone whose personal behaviour does not match their public persona. Check the left hand Head Line for behaviour in intimate relationships, and the right hand Head Line for work patterns and needs.

Check out 'Timing Techniques' for timing the numerous markings found on this line.

Palm Print 12
A curved Head Line

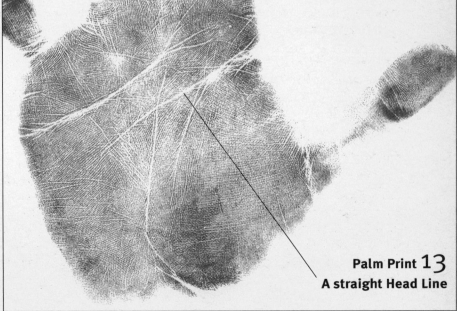

Palm Print 13
A straight Head Line

WITH A CURVED HEAD LINE WE WILL NEED TO:

- Express imagination and creativity

- Shoot from the hip; avoid complexities or intricacies

- Experiment with new ideas and take calculated risks

- Respond energetically and subjectively to problem-solving

With a curved Head Line we put our minds to being aggressively involved in life, and look for positions of authority.

At work, we aim to be:

- Creative, pro-active and results-driven high-flyers

- Seen as winners and are sensitive to criticism and failure

- Flexible, fast solution-finders

- Respected for our self-reliance and autonomy

- Fast decision-makers wanting to know only the bottom line

In relationships we:

- Should avoid looking to blame others

- Have quick flashes of temper

- Can detach easily from work problems

- Often communicate only when we need to solve large problems

- Expect romantic difficulties to be solved quickly

- Respond to others' problems by offering advice instead of empathy

- Need time alone to find our balance

WITH A STRAIGHT HEAD LINE WE WILL NEED TO:

- Take a rational, businesslike but unadventurous approach

- See proof before reaching conclusions

- Analyse using common-sense deductions

- Respond coolly and practically to problem-solving

With a straight Head Line we wish to be unflappable and unemotional in our responses, and can be shrewd and cunning when necessary.

At work, we aim to be:

- Practical, professional, business-minded and goal-driven

- Detached from our emotional needs

- Structured in organising our workload

- In a working relationship with others

- Aware of all the facts and possible outcomes before we act

In relationships we:

- Should avoid manipulating people or circumstances

- Are moody and can mull over problems for a long time

- Need time to unwind at night to forget stress at the office

- Need to communicate constantly with our partner

- Are silent only when suspicious or afraid of causing hurt

- Expect our partner to know how to help us automatically

- Need to be understood rather than to be offered solutions

- Want to share and explore our feelings before we clarify our priorities

Long or short?

Our Head Line brings to light our own rational or irrational responses; how we think with our heads and how we solve problems. Along with the finger length it determines how we process information. Understanding our Head Line unmasks the way in which we respond intellectually to life. Its length does not disclose the level of our intelligence but rather the length of our thinking process.

You should take into account the length of fingers (our analytical ability, see pages 34–6) and whether or not the Head Line is joined to the Life Line (indicating caution/recklessness, see page 57) before making assessments. A short Head Line is one that reaches no further than under the beginning of the ring finger. A long Head Line is one that extends towards the outer side of the palm, or has a deep long curve.

An extra-long Head Line

With an overly long Head Line we can be highly scientific, solve mind puzzles or be exasperatingly logical to the point of being blinkered. At worst we'll procrastinate endlessly. A Head Line that goes straight across the palm to the outer edge is known as the Sydney Line (see page 187) as it was discovered by medical researchers in Australia.

SYNTHESIS PART 2:
THE HEAD LINE AND LARGE HANDS

Check out the size of your hands compared with the length of your Head Line. This will show how long or short your fuse is! An impatient (short) Head Line would do a lot to offset the calm characteristics of large hands. Perhaps if you have this unusual mix you have an on-going battle to finish work, or you become easily frustrated with the length of time it takes to complete the projects you do so ably – knowing well enough that no-one else does them the way you do! A strong thumb or long index finger would also incline you towards positions of leadership, in which you would manage every aspect of business yourself. You would excel in business management or leadership where detail is the key to major success (noticing errors, finding loopholes, devising intricate strategies). Perhaps no-one would ever be good enough to take over from you upon retirement (there's an inability to give up control with a combination of these features) and you appear psychologically unable to delegate work to others! My father, who has very large hands for his build, has this combination and ran his firm with an extraordinary eye for detail until his early 80s. His preoccupation with the smaller matters, which others would overlook, spelt success for him in his field of legal work. A favourite quotation of his is sound advice for those of us with large hands: '97% of genius is the art of taking pains'.

A SHORT HEAD LINE REVEALS:

- A decisive, to-the-point, often impulsive mind

- An inability to notice the subtleties of a situation or problem

- An occasional lack of forethought or preparation

- A materialistic or specialist stance

- An abrupt manner when dealing with enquiries or problems

- A short attention span

For examples see pages 33 (top) and 91.

A LONG HEAD LINE REVEALS:

- Detailed thinking; well thought-out arguments and decisions; talkativeness

- An ability to tackle complex issues

- Slow thought processes but sustained powers of concentration

- Numerous hobbies and interests

- A thoughtful, considered manner when dealing with enquiries or problems

For examples see pages 130 and 133.

SYNTHESIS PART 3:
THE HEAD LINE AND SMALL HANDS

A long Head Line (one that reaches out further across the hand, ending under the little finger) will slow down your quickness of thought (as will long fingers with knotty joints, which add a questioning, analytical quality), but not of action. You can still move like greased lightning, but will be more careful in making decisions. This makes for a better manager of money, who can calculate risks. In business, with a short Head Line (only extending to a point below the ring finger) or a gap between the Head Line and Life Line, there could be recklessness and foolhardiness, betting everything on a risky outcome that could have been avoided or at least loss-adjusted. You have hunches about people and situations and the speed of your actions could see projects sail – or sink! Remember that success is when opportunity meets preparation. See the length and character of these lines in combination with the characteristics of the fingers to understand how you can best acheive your objectives. A long index finger gives you an added confidence to pioneer projects, whilst a noticeably short index finger stimulates you into proving to the world just how effective you can be on a large scale. A strong thumb adds to the decision-making abilities and sheer force of will, but with a weak thumb you should allow others to support your efforts. With the latter you should not carry the burden alone, but rather work with a balanced team of colleagues and be the one to direct the group on broader matters and the potential scope of the large-scale projects.

Delicate or coarse?

A delicate Head Line will show a delicate, somewhat fragile mentality. A coarse, thick Head Line reveals a blunt, brusque approach to solving problems – with this type of Head Line some of us choose to push our way through life by riding roughshod over others.

The start of the Head Line

One of the most important aspects of the Head Line is whether or not it is joined at its start to the Life Line. When the lines are not attached, we are self-reliant and develop our own opinions and sense of individuality from an early age and enjoy expressing our own mind. (Examples in this book can be found on pages 25 and 58.) Sometimes our independence is due to healthy parental neglect – our parents were busy or we had too many siblings! We had to look after ourselves, play on our own or act responsibly from early on. We possess spontaneity and a healthy degree of confidence (although a short index finger or an island in the Head Line would affect the level of self-confidence).

When the two lines are widely detached we can be too impulsive and conceited about our opinions, but others may envy our natural ability to express ourselves with dramatic flair. Unless we can maintain high principles and personal integrity we should avoid the cut and thrust of political life, remembering that absolute power corrupts absolutely.

When the Head Line is tied to the Life Line at its start we step carefully into new situations and make most decisions with caution. Where the two lines do not separate until some way down the line we can be a late-starter in life, often under parental control until well into our twenties. Often oversensitive, sometimes withdrawn, we have been happy to let others help us run our everyday life. Very often our parents were either over-protective or a little heavy-handed – self-confidence needed to be developed either way. If we have this line formation we should assume responsibility and face difficulties head-on, and should avoid slipping into co-dependent relationships, constantly seeking approval, or being non-committal in love affairs. (Examples can be found on pages 130 and 202.)

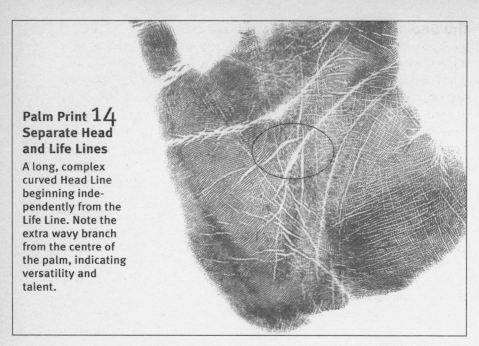

Palm Print 14
Separate Head and Life Lines

A long, complex curved Head Line beginning independently from the Life Line. Note the extra wavy branch from the centre of the palm, indicating versatility and talent.

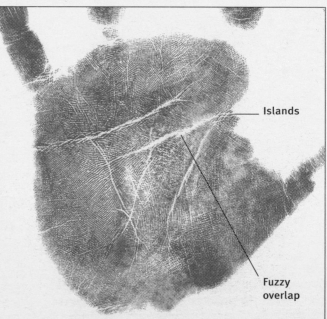

Palm Print 15
A Head Line linked to Life Line at their commencement

Here a straight, average length Head Line is lightly tied to the Life Line (both lines begin with islands). Note the fuzzy overlap in the late 20s and early 30s, when the owner of this palm print left her partner, began a new life, settled down and started a family.

Islands

Fuzzy overlap

The end of the Head Line

The place where the Head Line ends helps us to understand where we direct our thoughts and what we focus on when we're 'in our heads'. The usual ending is roughly an inch under the Heart Line, below the ring and little fingers (see Palm Print 15). It can also end in different types of fork – see page 196. When the Head Line ends in a curve up towards the little finger, we direct our thoughts towards money-making schemes (see Palm Print 16). When it curves down steeply into the palm or plummets towards the wrist, we prefer to submerge ourselves in a fantasy world in which we cannot be held accountable for the problems around us or where we feel numb to pain and hurt. When it ends in a star this can indicate that we fear losing control of our environment or our sanity.

We'll uncover other facets of the Head Line in the section 'Love, Health and Career'. In 'Timing Techniques' we'll see how markings on the Head Line affect our thought processes and reaction to stress, and we'll understand how the course of the Head Line vividly demonstrates our own method of thinking and how we develop ideas from A to B.

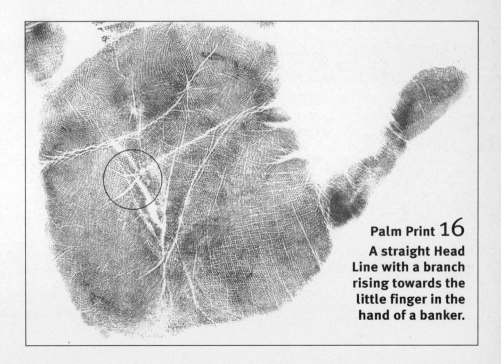

Palm Print 16

A straight Head Line with a branch rising towards the little finger in the hand of a banker.

The Heart Line: Our Emotional Response

Whereas the Head Line charts our particular way of dealing with life on a rational, logical level, the Heart Line discloses our emotional responses and capacity for affection. It registers the ups and downs of love – our romantic expectations, the manner in which we fall in love, the process of loving and being loved, and our reaction to heartbreak. It reveals the intensity of our emotional make-up and the strength of our sexual needs. Understanding our partner's Heart Line will help us to understand how best to approach them, communicate with them or seduce them, and how to understand their needs and expectations. *The more complex the line, the more complex the emotional reactions and sexual development.*

If you're unsure whether a Heart Line is straight or curved, place a ruler from the beginning of the Heart Line to its end and see whether it makes a noticeable bow. Some lines will extend in a straight direction but send branches up towards the index finger and vice versa. If yours is similarly complex take the direction of the most dominant branch or look at the general flow of the line and follow that course.

Interestingly, the more even or unmarked the line the more we are labelled 'cool, calm and collected' – this can hide a lack of interest in the emotions of others. This is particularly true where there are numerous even-sized chain formations along the Heart Line – we can be calculating and have more relaxed views on fidelity. A chained appearance is to be expected on most hands, revealing a healthy degree of compassion, sensitivity and vulnerability. If the line is fragile or poorly formed, it reveals great sensitivity to hurt. If the Heart Line is noticeably longer or deeper (particularly in a print) than the Head Line, our emotions dominate our thoughts and actions. Our heart rules our head. This is reversed if the Head Line is significantly longer or more dominant.

Curved or straight?

How do we express love and affection? What type of relationship are we looking for? To discover the answers to these questions we need to assess whether our Heart Lines are curved or straight.

> **Q: In Palm Print 17 there are a selection of straight and curved (and more complex) lines. Can you decide into which category these Heart Lines fall?**
> **(Answers overleaf.)**

**Palm Print 17
Curved and
straight Heart
Lines**

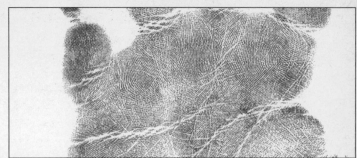

Palm A

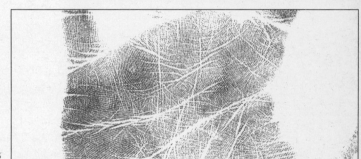

Palm B

Palm C

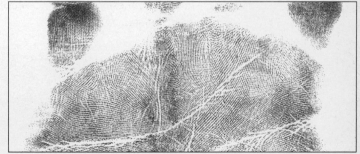

Palm D

The answers are:

Palm A: A straight, short, islanded, heavy Heart Line ending under the middle finger. Faint branches rising up to the middle finger ending in a 'V'-shaped heavy fork to the middle and index fingers. Low-set.

Palm B: A straight, short Heart Line with many fine descending lines, ending in a small fork. Low-set.

Palm C: A steeply curved Heart Line reaching up to the middle finger. High-set.

Palm D: A curved, long Heart Line reaching up to the index finger.

When reading the following summaries, be aware that you also need to take into account the complexity of the line and other hand features. How long is the line? (See page 64.) Does it send out branches? (See page 64.) Is the Mount of Venus strongly developed? (See page 42.) Does its shape (curved or straight) correspond to that of the Head Line? In addition, the left hand's Heart Line will show our more intimate and personal reactions, while the right hand shows our romantic expectations when socialising and dating.

WITH A CURVED HEART LINE WE:

- Are openly passionate, spontaneous and tactile
- Show emotion and affection in public
- Show our feelings through presents, surprises and spontaneous gestures
- Can be exhibitionist
- Release tension and open up through sex
- Like the see-saw and rough and tumble of relationships
- Enjoy making up after fiery arguments
- Seek warm, attractive, adventurous and outgoing partners
- Seek dominance, preferring to be 'on top' in a relationship

In general we are considered demonstrative. Look for strong, ruddy hands (and a reddish Heart Line) for warmth of character and for thumbs held away from the palms for candour (see page 85).

WITH A STRAIGHT HEART LINE WE:

- Are more analytical
- Prefer to show affection in private
- Show our feelings through words and recollections
- Need to shed any sexual inhibitions
- Seek agreement and harmony in relationships
- Seek quiet, sincere, thoughtful partners
- Seek equality or a receptive, supportive role in a relationship

Straight lines are found on those of us who are introverted and emotionally reserved. Remember, this does not automatically mean we are cold or unfeeling – look out for pale, narrow hands and an unblemished Heart Line for greater emotional detachment, and for thumbs held close to the palms for a reserved nature (see page 83).

How the shape of the Heart Line affects relationships

Although they say opposites attract, partnerships are often more successful if both have similar Heart Lines.

Seeking new relationships

Curved: We instigate relationships with enthusiasm and look for common ground; we need enthusiasm and look for early signs of sexual chemistry.
Straight: We wait for go-ahead signals, signs of good compatibility and then become involved; we need both emotional and mental chemistry.

When relationships begin

Curved: We are eager to impress, win over, commit and fall in love – although we are afraid of being rejected in our self-appointed role as 'pursuer'; we need to conquer but lose interest if our partner is too available or needy; we need feedback and appreciation.
Straight: We seek to understand our partner's deeper feelings and share responsibilities; we intuitively understand how to maintain the relationship's equilibrium; we feel content when our partner is happy; we need appreciation for our many unspoken gestures.

Sexual needs

Curved: We want self-satisfaction; we act spontaneously and feel rejected if our partner does not want sex immediately; we would benefit from learning to trust our partner enough to explore our more passive side.
Straight: We need to feel wanted before intimacy; we look for sexual confidence in others and seek reassurance, time and trust; we cleverly steer the sexual situation; we would benefit from learning to have the courage to ask that our needs be met and to play out a more dominant role.

Encountering problems

Curved: We face difficulties head-on and then want to forget them; we expect situations to resolve easily; we need time away to recharge our batteries and then we take up where we left off.
Straight: We are reactive; we fret and consider the long-term implications, keeping them in the back of our mind; we need indications of the relationship's permanence during difficulties; we seek to manipulate situations through emotional blackmail.

Expressing anger

Curved: We explode, shout, throw things, then forget; we would benefit from learning to consider the harmful effects of rash actions or unthinking remarks.
Straight: We sulk, suffer in silence or frustration; we resort to passive aggression; we would benefit from learning to release anger without feeling guilt.

Ending relationships

Curved: We usually make the first move to end them; we confront differences and move on.
Straight: We worry, letting it affect our moods, eating and sleeping habits; we find it difficult to let go.

The end of the Heart Line

The ending of the Heart Line discloses the way we react to potential partnerships and to emotional hurt. The most common ending is between the index and middle fingers (often with a small fork), indicating average emotional and sexual reactions and a healthy capacity for love and commitment. If we have this ending, we would benefit from learning to be more communicative with our partners and trusting them enough to let them know our feelings, doubts and insecurities on a regular basis.

When the line ends in a small fork this shows a balance between our practical and emotional sides. With a larger fork or numerous branches we have

WITH A LONG HEART LINE ENDING DIRECTLY UNDER THE INDEX FINGER WE:	WITH A SHORT HEART LINE ENDING BELOW THE MIDDLE FINGER WE:
• Want to believe the best of everyone	• Can often be cynical about people and love
• Have high standards in love; are idealistic, selective and hard to please	• Are more pragmatic about expectations of love and commitment
• Look for the knight in shining armour (or princess to rescue)	• May prefer to operate on a sexual rather than an emotional level
• Need to be more realistic with our expectations	• Should make efforts to be less judgemental, quick to judge or selfish
• Put friends and lovers on a pedestal but...	• Should put past hurts and insecurities behind us
• ...Feel disappointed and let-down when they fall off!	• Wish to control our emotional responses to protect ourselves
• Act generously to win over others	• Are sometimes afraid of never finding true love

a more complex sexuality and may not be as much in control of our emotions and sexuality as we would like to believe. We may flirt, tease or play with others' feelings without regard for the consequences.

Do we cynically expect disappointment or long for that knight in shining armour? If we chart the course of the Heart Line (from under the little finger towards the index finger) we can uncover important clues to our expectations in relationships. Does the line end prematurely, does it curve downwards or does it reach up in expectation towards the base of the index finger?

Is the Heart Line high-set or low-set? See page 144 for more details.

Discover various other types of Heart Line in the section 'Love, Health and Career'.

 ## SYNTHESIS PART 4:
A SHORT HEART LINE – CURVED OR STRAIGHT?

When assessing a short Heart Line, note whether the line is curved or straight. With a curved Heart Line ending under the middle finger you will explore physical passion without much discrimination or without wishing to be involved emotionally. Or perhaps you cannot be reached emotionally (look for these signs on a print, see page 154). Sensual and highly sexual, in the pursuit of physical pleasure you can be consumed by the act of sex often without wanting emotional ties. One client with this line was a masseur who felt he had found his niche being paid for sex and massage. A straight Heart Line terminating under the middle finger may not be as keen to pursue sex, finding other ways to release their energy. (For examples see pages 58 (bottom) and 164.)

SYNTHESIS PART 5:
DIFFERENCES BETWEEN THE LEFT AND RIGHT HEART LINES

Note any differences between both Heart Lines. A Heart Line ending under the middle finger on the left hand will reveal a cynical attitude to romance because of hurt and self-protectiveness (or perhaps because of a failed parental marriage). But if the line extends to the index finger on our right hand, we still employ very high standards and aim to meet the perfect match. If this combination of hand and line is reversed, we believe in true love and the stuff of dreams but put up an emotional wall so potential partners cannot reach us, and we don't expect people ever to match our expectations.

The Simian Line: A Law unto Ourselves

The Simian Line is a fascinating variant of the Head and Heart Lines. It appears like a railway track formation extending for some distance across the hand replacing these separate lines. If we understand that the Heart Line embodies our emotional responses and the Head Line rules our analytical capacities, we can see that one line merging the head and heart is likely to result in a one-track approach to life, unable to separate emotion from logic. This was one reason why old palmistry books attributed savage impulses, aggression and brutality to those with this line. More typically we alternate between being too rational and too emotional. I was taught that this is the sign of the genius or the idiot; there's some truth in this, as there is little middle ground in any area of life for those with a Simian Line.

When the line is found on the left hand our emotional make-up is often so complex that we find great difficulty in feeling satisfied with or at peace in a relationship. We need a superhero who is perfect and yet able to tolerate and forgive our own short-comings. I liken the meaning of this line to the astrological sign of Scorpio and have found it in the hands of people whose horoscopes have Scorpio or Taurus prominent and the planet Uranus highlighted.

Approximately half of those with Down's Syndrome will have a Simian Line in at least one palm. For the rest of us, Simian Lines in both hands will display more of the characteristics listed below than when the line is present in one hand only. As with the example prints, there are often strands of the Head or Heart Line present on a hand with a Simian Line.

With the Simian Line we:

- Stand out from the crowd for our single-mindedness and intensity
- Have tunnel vision and determination to pursue our excellent ideas
- Employ our own method of doing things; are a law unto ourselves
- Believe in what we do 100%; have remarkable powers of concentration
- Have black-or-white personalities, believing people and opinions are either right or wrong
- Exude charisma, energy and strength (often both physical and mental)
- Find it hard to relax and often feel tense
- Can be intensely religious or feel on a mission
- May stay obstinately in situations until the bitter end
- Need to direct our energies to constructive work
- Are obsessive-compulsive personalities
- Have extreme, all-or-nothing characters; others have extreme reactions to us, too

Palm Print 18 Examples of Simian Lines

Palm A: Hand print of an energetic woman in her sixties who is determined to live a full life

Palm B: Hand print of an off-beat and intense lawyer

Palm C: A semi-Simian Line on the print of a successful financial market analyst

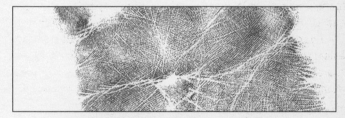

Palm D: Hand print of a man with heart disease

- Can be ruthlessly efficient dictators when in positions of power and make tough opponents
- Are single-minded and sometimes merciless, particularly in eliminating those who oppose us
- Need to control our environment and to win and succeed
- Can enjoy sexual extremes and aggression
- Are capable of greatness and originality (particularly when the line is on the right hand)

SYNTHESIS PART 6:
DIRECTING SIMIAN CHARACTERISTICS

To discover how the Simian person can best utilise what this vital feature represents, take into account their fingers, finger prints, the Fate Line and, most importantly, the size of their thumb. The element of the hand shape will reveal where the energy is directed (e.g. Earth: towards physical pursuits). Sometimes the Fate Line will appear weak, as though the driving force comes from the character rather than obligations (Fate Line). Healthwise, Simian-people need to be careful of becoming workaholics and neglecting their bodies, particularly their hearts.

The Fate Line: Our Direction

The course, strength and direction of the Fate Line depicts our goals, ambitions, responsibilities and tasks. It represents our life path – whatever motivates us to get out of bed each morning. The Fate Line is known to develop on children's hands at the age when they begin to sense their role outside the home or when teenagers discover certain responsibilities they have to the people around them. A strong Fate Line on a very young child's hand reveals an early understanding of what is expected of them, a sense of the family unit, an eagerness to please and perhaps a problem with developing independence.

While a change of job may be reflected in the Fate Line, it is important to note that not all our job changes will show as breaks, overlaps or new developments on the Fate Line, but *significant changes in perspective and attitude towards the life path* will be found on the line corresponding to the times these occur.

Although concerned with our individual journey in life, the Fate Line also tells of our links with others, for invariably our work involves a level of interaction – whether our path is one of a teacher, athlete, waiter, parent, politician or civil servant. For many who think of a partnership as their main role in life, the Fate Line represents the most important personal relationship(s), so often a spouse is represented by the dominant Fate Line. Again, as with the other lines, the shape, strength and direction of the line reveal both events in our life and our attitude to our working responsibilities.

Strong or fragmented?

Look to see whether the Fate Line is strong and unbroken, or whether it is light and fragmented.

Palm Print 19
Examples of Fate Lines

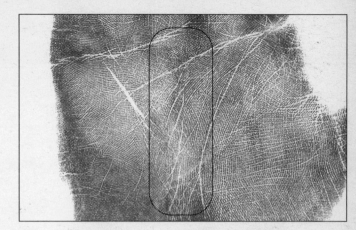

Palm A

Numerous, feathery Fate Lines

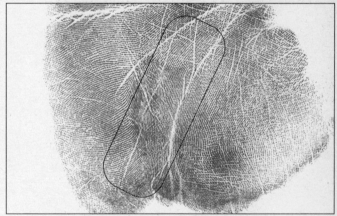

Palm B

A light Fate Line with strands; it doubles up when a new line rises from the Life Line (see page 192)

Palm C

A long, unbroken and strong Fate Line; it is lighter in between the Head and Heart Lines

AN UNBROKEN, STRONG FATE LINE REVEALS:

- A steady working life or purposeful climb up the job ladder
- Set goals and plans; we know where we are going
- A duty-bound and responsible approach to life and work commitments
- Perseverance; we are undeterred by setbacks or interference

It can also indicate a rather uneventful, dull life path where very few risks are taken. We do what is expected of us or simply follow in the family footsteps.

A LIGHT OR FRAGMENTED FATE LINE REVEALS:

- Many work, personal or home changes; a low boredom threshold
- A lack of focus; we can be indecisive, vague or distracted
- A less settled life and dislike of routine; we are often anxious about the future
- A malleable personality; we fear being unable to actualise goals

It can also denote that we cannot be relied upon to complete jobs. We dislike 9 to 5 work – perhaps our personal dramas impinge upon work time or our heart is not in our work.

A missing Fate Line

The Fate Line is a good significator of our place in society – of where and how we fit in (or wish to fit in). A non-conformist may not have much of a Fate Line. It is rarely absent in the hands of the homeless, as some books have suggested, because a missing Fate Line is more indicative of the following:

- An independent or wayward spirit; no set direction, routine or pattern in life
- A drop-out
- Rebellion against the expectations of family or society
- A life of adventure not bound by confines of routine or circumstance
- We who are a law unto ourselves

Check out 'Timing Techniques' for information on timing this line and on how to recognise major events on the line.

QUICK QUIZ 2

1. Which line governs our emotional make-up?

2. If we avoid routine or obligations, which line will be relatively faint?

3. Which markings indicate a planned change?

4. Which marking suggests protection during an uneasy transition?

5. Which sign indicates lethargy or a negative attitude to life?

6. What indicates a practical, business-minded approach to work?

7. Who is more able to tackle complex information – the person with a short or the person with a long Head Line?

8. Who prefers to pursue and conquer new partners in relationships – the person with a curved or the person with a straight Heart Line?

9. Which marking betrays intensity and single-mindedness?

10. A steady climb up the professional ladder is more likely to be seen in which type of Fate Line?

(Answers in Appendix 3, page 218.)

Step 3
The Fingers and the Thumb

Expressing Our Character

The length of the fingers is determined in the womb and is an excellent indicator of how we grasp and process information. We explored this on pages 34–6. In addition to this, each finger governs a particular area of expression and our personality. A finger that dominates the hand will dominate the character with its associated personality traits.

Look at your hand and compare the length of the fingers. Is one particularly long or heavy? In most cases the middle finger will be the longest, but perhaps the index finger is powerful, or the ring finger exceeds the index and is rigidly erect? Perhaps all your fingers are average in length but your powerful thumb dominates the hand. Sometimes the little finger stands out by being thick, long or curved. Perhaps the middle finger is significantly short.

Look too to see if any finger is held straighter than the rest. This may show the type of belief systems or principles that dominate your thoughts. Even when arthritis has set in, those fingers that remain straight can be clear indicators of a determination to continue the pursuits ruled by that particular finger.

- A straight index finger shows a strong moral stance and integrity.
- A straight middle finger reveals a responsible nature.
- A straight ring finger shows creativity and that the pursuit of applause and attention is a motivating factor.
- A straight little finger can show a strong need to be heard.

The Dominant Digit

If one of our digits dominates the others (by being noticeably long, short, heavy, straight, inclined, etc.) then the keywords shown in Palm Print 20 will identify how we seek to express our character.

Palm Print 20
Characteristics of dominant digits

MIDDLE

Anxious, austere, conscientious, dutiful, faithful, hesitant, industrious, introverted, methodical, modest, pessimistic, prudent, reserved, rigid, self-doubting, serious
Astrologically: Saturn

RING

Affable, artistic, benevolent, considerate, cultured, depressed, entertaining, flattering, glory-seeking, gracious, indiscreet, lazy, refined, stylish, vain
Astrologically: Sun and Venus

LITTLE

Analytical, articulate, cunning, eloquent, expressive, juvenile, manipulative, perceptive, persuasive, sarcastic, talkative
Astrologically: Mercury

INDEX

Ambitious, argumentative, authoritative, caustic, controlling, dramatic, enterprising, imperious, independent, influential, optimistic, powerful, self-determining, self-willed, stubborn, tyrannical
Astrologically: Jupiter

THUMB

Adventurous, aggressive, audacious, combative, courageous, dynamic, energetic, enthusiastic, explosive, hard-headed, impatient, incisive, indomitable, indefatigable, obstinate, powerful, pushy, strong-willed
Astrologically: Mars

The Thumb – The Chief

This is certainly the most important digit on the hand. It reveals our drive, willpower and the extent of our forcefulness. It is a measure of our self-control as well as our need to control our environment and the people around us. A thumb that is unusual in its shape or impressive in its size will always stamp its mark on the personality, and thus should be taken strongly into consideration when assessing the character.

Strong or weak?

A strong thumb is one that is solid, broad, stands out impressively on its own, and (when held towards the hand) reaches at least half way up the bottom section of the index finger. With a long, strong thumb we need to be someone special, to be recognised as a forceful character and a strong personality and need to feel capable and effective. We can do almost anything we put our minds to. We are dominating, independent, commanding people who assume roles of authority. We aim to impress people, but can be surprisingly impressionable ourselves. It is important to remember that *a strong thumb can accomplish much and can take its owner far, regardless of any difficulties displayed in the palm lines.*

A short, thin or generally weak-looking thumb (as compared to the rest of the hand and fingers) can point to problems of self-control as well as an inability to put our ideas into action. A weak thumb can negate the potential found in palm lines, so it is important to exercise self-control and willpower, and to develop forcefulness and self-confidence. As Calvin Coolidge said, 'Nothing is more common than unrewarded talent.'

The tip

With a strong thumb tip (one that is larger than the lower phalange) we are decisive 'doers', able to accomplish much through willpower, self-motivation and sheer force of personality. When the tip is too thick, we can be the type who uses a sledgehammer to crack a nut! We could learn a lot from a subtle approach to life's problems. (There's another blunt tip known as the Clubbed Thumb; find more about this and how to recognise it on pages 156–7.)

When the tip is small, we need to develop greater staying power and become more decisive and less dependent on the thoughts of others, but until we acheive this we should work with others to formulate plans and fulfil our ambitions.

The more supple the tip, the more we are able to adapt to life's surprises. A stiff thumb tip betrays a stubborn personality unable to move with the times.

Sometimes the tip of the thumb is naturally bent backwards to a noticeable degree. With this we are truly generous to a fault and sometimes don't know when enough is enough. We are extravagant and find it hard to walk out of shops without using our credit card. I had a friend who possessed this characteristic and who worked in a famous London department store. When she was paid each week, she would spend most of her wages, taking advantage of her employee's discount, before she found her way out of the store!

The lower phalange

When the lower phalange (the lower section) of the thumb is longer than the tip, we have many ideas and are able to develop these logically through our intellect, particularly if we also have long fingers and a long Head Line. The longer this section, the better we are at analysing situations and responding with reason and logical thought. The time we take to prepare before tackling tasks enables us to foresee and side-step obstacles from the outset. If the phalange is substantially longer than the tip, we do better as ideas people, motivating others to carry out the ideas we conceive or convincing people to buy these ideas for future development.

A short lower phalange and long thumb tip belong to those of us who have the necessary push to accomplish much (including selling directly to the public) but should leave the idea development to others. When this lower section is too thick, we can lack diplomacy to the point of alienating others around us. When it is rather thin, we sometimes lack common sense but can be reassuring and tactful (often hiding our true feelings about a situation).

Of course, the ideal would be to have both sections balanced – to be able to reason and to carry out our plans without relying on brute force.

Newly-born infants who hold out their thumbs from the first day are displaying early signs of their strong character and an eagerness to get acquainted with their new surroundings. When thumbs stay close to the hand or are curled into the palm for longer than a few days after birth, this is a considered a sign that the child may be delicate. In addition, nurses can sometimes tell the strength of a patient's will to live by the position of their thumbs: thumbs held out may show that they are battling on.

The Index Finger – The General

The index finger, its shape, length, current position relative to the other fingers, and its finger print all reveal vital clues to our ego, self-image, vanity and ambition. It is symbolic of the person we take out into the world and represents our public face (on the right hand) as well as our personal manner (left hand). Along with the thumb it is a defining part of who we really are. The index finger governs our personal beliefs as well as providing clues to our personal interests. It is very self-orientated and self-directed. It also shows the extent of our:

- self-confidence
- self-awareness
- leadership ability
- sense of authority
- self-esteem
- pride
- ability to soldier on with positive self-conviction

When the index finger is of average length (of similar stature to the ring finger) we exhibit these traits in moderation and with a healthy balance. Check the Head Line as well, as islands or severe disruptions on this line will make it more of a challenge to realise these traits fully.

With a long index finger (one that is longer than the ring finger), we need to take charge of our lives (this transition may not happen fully until we have reached the age of 29 or 30, though). We often have a parental instinct towards others, and need to have the same protection from our loved ones in return. We have a healthy ego, fuelled by a desire to be seen as special, or to 'play God' or the good Samaritan. We like to take charge of situations and can be somewhat of a general marshalling his troops. We should avoid excessive vanity as well as instinct to control events and people around us. The long index finger can be one of the signs of a diva temperament. We can be imperious and think we are better than others ('I wish others didn't act so superior. It makes it much more difficult for those of us who naturally are'). A pointed tip to the finger adds bossiness and hen-pecking. In addition, our religion tends to be a private matter and we sense a deep connection with God, without necessarily following one rigid system of beliefs or another.

When the index finger is short (shorter than the ring finger), our instinct is to

> ### Synthesis Part 7:
> ### Differences between the left and right index fingers
>
> Remember to apply the meanings of finger length to whichever hand has the long or short index finger for signs of the characteristics being displayed personally (left hand) or professionally (right hand). In addition, some of you may have one short index finger and one long. If short on the left hand and long on the right, you present a bold front to the world at large, but may hide secret fears or insecurities. Only in relationships or with family members do these surface. Many people fall in love with a person who exhibits confidence and a successful image, only encountering the fragile ego in private later. When the left hand has the longer index finger, you can take comfort from the fact of having had a secure grounding personally (probably from a secure home-life and childhood). However, it may require effort to translate this confidence into the public arena and assert yourself at work, particularly where public speaking is concerned.

prove ourselves to the world. Others may label this a Napoleon complex because we may have a sense that we are inferior, not good enough or a failure. We may feel shy or timid in social situations (or, if the short finger is on the left hand, unable to be assertive in personal relationships), and in order to combat this we make strong efforts to be seen as someone important. At other times we battle to maintain confidence and keep our spirits up. Situations sometimes appear to conspire against us and we feel forced to take the blame for others' problems. We must learn to be accountable for our own actions only, and understand that we will succeed when we face our personal and professional responsibilities.

In either case, whether the index finger is noticeably long or short, there is a fear of failure that drives us. We have doubts that are often masked by bravado.

The Middle Finger – The Upstanding Citizen

This finger, unless deformed or curved significantly, literally and figuratively holds up the hand. Along with its finger print, size and inclination, it tells us of our attitude to duties and responsibilities. It holds the answers to questions such as: are we serious about life and the commitments we make? Can we hold down a job and be relied upon? Where do our responsibilities lie?

When the Middle finger is noticeably long (almost standing head and shoulders above the other fingers) we are good judges of what is right and wrong. We can be effective critics at work and scientific in our methodology, evaluating situations, taking charge of research projects and keeping standards high. We are faithful, controlled, reliable and responsible, although we need to make it clear to others that we enjoy our own company and may not always be in the mood for socialising. We take life seriously, have a strong conscience and can be introverted and introspective. We may also be materialistic. When very long, this finger can reflect a morbid nature; the lonely and depressive side to our character.

When this finger is noticeably short (only slightly longer than both the ring and index fingers) this is a strong clue that we do not like responsibility or the rules laid down by others. If it is accompanied by a short or absent Fate Line, we may have dropped out in some way, perhaps at college, from the rat race or from society in general. The key is, perhaps, to stick with situations – taking time to avoid making rash decisions or quitting a situation when the going gets tough – or to begin to view the situation from a different angle. If commitment and responsibility are not our strong points, we should avoid jobs and personal relationships that require a rigid set of rules. A visit to the Latin countries could easily convince us that some successful careers can be made out of the pursuit of pleasure and with the avoidance of routine!

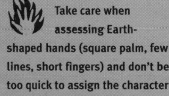

Take care when assessing Earth-shaped hands (square palm, few lines, short fingers) and don't be too quick to assign the character associations of finger length. The fingers will often look similar in size, even the little finger. The middle finger may appear deceptively short, too.

The Ring Finger – The Performer

This finger rules creative and artistic pursuits, and shows the measure of our interest in these matters. The length of this finger indicates whether or not we can put ourselves out on display in the public arena, particularly on stage.

The ring finger is traditionally associated with taking risks, and indeed gamblers and those of us who thrive in jobs with adventure generally have long ring fingers. (For challenges and overcoming obstacles, employ those with a long index finger!) Another quality inherent when the ring finger is longer than the index finger is a creative instinct – we are able to apply our talents to any given situation and make the most of it. Many actors (particularly the uninhibited ones) have long and (often) very straight ring fingers. The need for applause, adulation and recognition is paramount.

> Men with longer ring fingers than index fingers are, according to research at the University of Liverpool's School of Biological Sciences, more fertile (see page 163). The team have also found that the longer the ring finger (as compared to the index) the greater the body–eye co-ordination. The scientists, headed by Dr John Manning, found this feature in top professional footballers, gifted young musicians, mathematicians and others who had proven excellent in tests of spatial awareness or in jobs which required this skill.

Yet the length of this finger alone does not reveal talent. Whorls and a distinctive Head Line point to a particular innate talent, which we may choose to develop. With a long ring finger we prefer the influence and respect that acclaim brings, rather than the benefits of power and money (the index finger). The love of applause far exceeds the lonely pursuit of power, and we seek money only to provide a comfortable lifestyle. Above all our nature is a creative one, and opportunities in these areas will be met with enthusiasm.

With a long ring finger we also seek to understand ourselves through self-expression and like to see concrete results of our efforts (particularly if the Head Line is straight). We aim to be available, charming and pleasant. If others want absolute sincerity or the bottom-line truth, they should ask those with a long index finger. With a long ring finger we may embellish the facts to provide a pleasant atmosphere, preferably one in which we can glow uninterrupted. A love of clothes and accessories and an in-built understanding of personal style can also accompany a long ring finger.

A short ring finger is quite rare. It can indicate a Philistine attitude to works of art ('Why did they bother?') and creative pursuits in general. With a short ring finger we need to develop spontaneity and shed inhibitions. I've found these people can be very private (particularly if they lead a public life), and there will be shyness – dread even – about being on stage or performing of any kind. If you find a rare example of a performer with a short ring finger, expect their motivation to be other than fame or even applause. With a short ring finger we are certainly not the ones selling our story to the tabloid newspaper. Our private life is considered sacrosanct and we avoid self-promotion.

The Little Finger – The Communicator

Perhaps the most intriguing of all the digits, the little finger governs exchange of all kinds: sexual, financial, business and commercial. It provides us with a good clue as to possible parental problems or obsessions and how we relate to family and partners.

When the little finger is long (reaching halfway up the nail section of the ring finger), we are loquacious people, expert at persuading, influencing or manipulating others. We have the gift of the gab and could make a successful salesperson or trickster. Often there is innate writing or speaking ability. Be aware that sometimes a long little finger appears short because it is low-set on the hand (see pages 87–8).

When the little finger is short or appears delicate alongside the other fingers, we may carry shyness into adulthood, avoiding eye contact or public events where we have to meet and mingle with many people. When we feel at ease in company we can be witty and versatile. Emotionally we can be late developers and we need to learn to spend more time articulating our feelings in partnerships. Sometimes emotionally or sexually immature, we look at romance through rose-tinted glasses and expect the endings promised in fairytales. We need to develop greater self-understanding in how we respond to close friendships and partnerships. We are easily disappointed by problems in love and can be touchy and over-react to criticism (particularly if the Heart Line ends under the index finger). It is this childlike, ingenuous attitude, however, that makes us excellent parents or teachers of young children. We share an affinity with children and are able to relate to them on their level and communicate with them effectively. We understand their instincts, expectations and reactions better than do other adults. I've seen this feature on the hands of a number of nursery teachers and children's television presenters.

Andrew Fitzherbert, in his book *Hand Psychology*, looked at this feature in detail. He found those of us with short little fingers to have:

- immature responses in partnerships
- a youthful appearance and enthusiasm for life
- an inability to control negative emotions
- strong reactions to minor irritations

The Three Phalanges of Every Finger

As we have seen, there is much information to be gained from studying the fingers, and some of it is complex. This section, however, is very easy to remember. Forget the thumb for a moment. Each finger has three sections, called phalanges and each phalange rules a level of consciousness. The length of the phalanges may be deceptive to the eye, so you may wish to measure the length of each finger section (from the palm, not the back of the hand).

Top phalange

The top (nail) phalange points to our higher spiritual desires. When the top section is the longest on all or most of our eight fingers, we are religious, often in our own quiet way, and we question – and seek to understand – the meaning of life. Look to a long index finger to emphasise this. (Interestingly, the hands of leaders and evangelists of organised religion usually don't show the signs of religiosity – they tend to have Earth-shaped, materialistic hands.) When the phalange is shorter, we have little interest in what goes on outside our own personal sphere.

Middle phalange

The middle phalange relates to our organisational skills, as well as any practical business acumen. When this is the longest section, we aim to compete and survive in a business climate. Look to a straight Head Line or an Earth hand to add weight to this analysis. When this phalange is short, we have difficulty organising our financial affairs and struggle to work effectively or consistently with proven time management systems.

Lower phalange

The lower (base) phalange corresponds to our most basic needs, comforts and desires. When it is the most dominant section of the fingers, we can be hedonistic or self-indulgent, particularly with food, clothes, possessions, drink and sex. We may never throw things away and have clutter around us. An Earth hand will support this feature, as will few lines on the palm. This section is rarely significantly short, but if it is found to be it can signify that we may neglect our physical side to the detriment of our health. A more common trait is that the lower phalange appears pinched in at the bottom of the section – it's the sign of the fussy eater.

A few years ago a client arrived at my office and announced that she had a dilemma in her life which was causing her great stress. The problem lay in that she and her family had decided that she must follow her religious vocation (which had been revealed to her some years before), yet she had secretly begun a sexual relationship with a man and found she could not give up the physical side. She struggled with the idea of relinquishing sex and her clandestine affair. Were her basic desires stronger than her commitments to her ordained religious life path? During the consultation she spoke at length of her religious obligations, but the one feature in her hands that threw light upon her predica-ment was a short top (nail) phalange combined with an overdeveloped lower (base) phalange on each finger.

Masculine and Feminine Qualities

Examining the traits of the index and ring fingers, we would be forgiven for auto-matically assuming the index finger is wholly a 'masculine' influence and the ring finger has 'feminine' attributes. Yet most of my clients with long index fingers, regardless of their gender, have a greater understanding of their 'feminine' qualities – they are more naturally attuned to this side. They do, however, make efforts to project strong personality traits usually labelled 'masculine' and strive for 'masculine' rewards. The opposite occurs with those with long ring fingers: they have a natural 'masculine' influence and many seek to balance this by developing their receptive, 'feminine' side. It appears that a dominant index or ring finger motivates us to seek to harmonise innate traits with the opposite principles to achieve a male–female balance.

On average, men's ring fingers tend to be slightly longer than their index fingers, whereas in women the two fingers tend to be the same length. Long ring fingers suggest that higher levels of testosterone were present at a crucial period in the development of the lungs, brain and heart, whereas scientists associate the development of long index fingers with oestrogen and luteinising hormone (both critical for female reproduction).

When looking at the lines of the hand, generally speaking, with regard to the Head Line and Heart Line, straight lines are more feminine' in character (more thoughtful, sensitive, calculating), whilst curved lines are more 'masculine' (action-orientated).

The Creative Curve (a noticeable curve of the outer edge of the hand from the little finger downwards) is a 'feminine' attribute adding creativity, intuition, softness, sensitivity to criticism and empathy.

I was intrigued to find a long, pointed index finger on the hand of American pro-wrestler-turned-Governor Jesse Ventura. His hands-on style in both the political and entertain-ment arenas demonstrated the natural no-nonsense, 'take charge' approach of the index finger, but what of the feminine angle? Another photo revealed his flamboyant sense of style, the showman adorned in feathers and pink outfits for his former profession. The index finger revealed the complexities of both sides of this man.

Finger Positioning – The Party Piece

Would you like to be able to grasp accurate facts about your friends instantly, without even looking at their palms? We can gain some fascinating insights into current problems or situations simply by assessing the relative positions of the fingers and thumb. We can do this by asking them to shake their hands and hold them up towards us or lay them gently on a table palm side up. Then look at the positions of the fingers and thumb and relate them to the positions listed below. Bear in mind, though, that *most of the finger positioning can be temporary, reflecting current situations*. The relative positions of the fingers and thumbs will change as a person's self-confidence grows or diminishes, as they shed inhibitions, need more freedom in their relationships and so on. The following are the most telling of the signs that are revealed. Some of them can be seen in Palm Print 21.

a. Thumb held close to the palm

We are feeling insecure or afraid of others' judgements. We need to pull back.
We need our privacy respected and give very little personal information away (astrologically we might find secretive Scorpio or reserved Saturn dominant in the horoscope). We are guarded and self-contained, and feel challenged when expected to socialise. We may have a handful of friends who know us well; the rest are acquaintances who think they are on more familiar terms. All others see is what we wish them to see – just the tip of the iceberg. Others will only get to know us if we let them in to our private world. It really is by invitation only. The message that comes across is 'Respect my personal life; don't get too close or risk losing me'. Our personal space is important.

Hand analyst Ed Campbell notes that these are people who establish personal boundaries, can say 'no' to others, and reject unacceptable behaviour from people. I would suggest this comes into play later in life, particularly when the Head Line leaves the Life Line or strengthens. Of course, such discrimination can result in us being branded difficult, uptight or selfish. One can only speculate how many women in the workplace are labelled 'bitches' because, with this hand feature, they are more self-determined and less dependent on the approval of others.

With a weak thumb, we can, at worst, be deceitful and weak-willed (particularly if the thumb tip curls into the hand).

When the left thumb is held in closer than the right thumb, our personal life is strictly off limits, but we have learned to be more sociable, outgoing and familiar with people on a day-to-day basis.

It is rare to see the right thumb held closer than the left, but when it is,

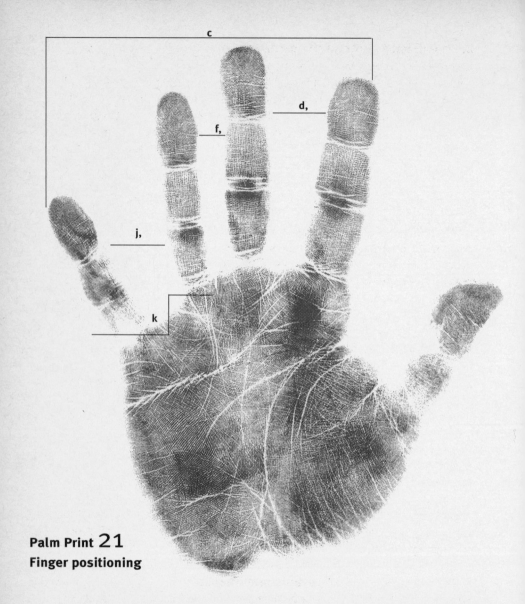

Palm Print 21
Finger positioning

others can expect us to be comfortable in our own surroundings but we feel the world is a scary place. Both thumbs tend to relax and move away from the hand when we feel more confident with people in our personal (left hand) or public (right hand) roles. Learning to trust loved ones will usually be a major step in learning to relax.

b. Thumb held out from the palm

We are feeling at ease with others and self-confident.

We are generous and open to the people who matter to us. We are also natural performers and could tell you our life story at the drop of a hat. What you see is generally what you get, and we want to impress people with our exuberance and sociable behaviour. We can, at the same time, be too self-involved and wish to dominate the conversation with our own stories. Others can recognise in us the monologue-giver: 'That's enough about me. Let's talk about you. What do you think of me?'

Again, Ed Campbell has some revealing insights here. He states that with this thumb position we have difficulty with personal boundaries, with ending bad relationships and saying 'no' to others. It is, he asserts, the classic sign of the co-dependent. If we have this thumb position, we will, of course, need to establish ground-rules if we choose work as a therapist or in any other situation where others depend on us for support.

c. Index and little fingers both positioned 'off the hand' (i.e. jutted out away from the other fingers)

We don't want to be hemmed in and want to rebel against frustrating or restricting circumstances.

We are unconventional in our lives and need to find our own rhythm in relationships and our own working pace. We also enjoy our own company. Others may call us bohemian, but we make efforts to be sociable on our own off-beat terms.

d. Index finger jutted out away from the hand

We are feeling confident, bold and keen to get what we want.

We aim to assert our needs and be seen as self-determining. We like to be in charge and to map out our own life. Others find it almost impossible to direct or advise us, as we have such strong opinions about the way in which we want to run our life. Relationships can be difficult if our partner cannot accept our consuming passion for independence.

e. Index finger slanted towards middle finger

We are feeling unsociable, shy or bothered.

It's likely that we need reassurance from loved ones, or would rather remain involved with the home than branch out on our own. We feel quite insecure about where to take our life and how to go about achieving our ambitions at this point in time.

f. Ring and middle fingers held close together

We must dedicate some time to our own projects in this period. Although we may be enjoying time on our own, we may also be feeling particularly insecure about the future and afraid of making it on our own.

This is a classic sign of being bound up with responsibilities and worries about what others think and their expectations of us. Sometimes these responsibilities are towards a loved one, maybe an old or infirm family member, but there seems to be a touch of martyrdom. We may be the one in the family who has given up our time to look after the sick relative, for example. In some ways we enjoy sacrifice, but we may suffer long-term unless we make time for our own needs. Family and duty may come first for a while, but when we feel less guilty we could run amok – or find a secret way of expressing our individuality. Sexually there may be a fear of letting go and enjoying the physical act of lovemaking.

When these two fingers are close, we must try to explore particular avenues that can bring us personal satisfaction without feeling guilty for having a good time. When the middle finger has developed a noticeable curve towards the ring finger, the situation has been going on for a number of years and should be addressed now.

g. Ring finger held far from middle finger

We need to enjoy time off without losing sight of personal goals.

This is a sign that we need our own space and enjoy time away from family or job responsibilities.

h. Little finger curled in on itself

Sex and physical intimacy may scare us at the moment.

When we hold our little finger in this way it appears almost hesitant and shy. This finger relates to matters of communication, particularly to sex and relationships, so we must remain choosy but be bolder. When it naturally curls back into the hand, we may be feeling unsure of our sexual self and how we can relate intimately to others. There may also be prudishness from a Victorian attitude in the home.

i. Little finger inclined towards ring finger, appearing crooked

First check if this is due to arthritis or an accident. If not, the following should apply. We who have a curved little finger are canny about money and business.

Our shrewdness could even develop into cutting corners with our tax return or looking for ways to make a fast buck. Others may call us deceitful or on the make.

j. Little finger jutted out away from the palm

We need time to ourselves, away from past hurt or loved ones who wish to hen-peck, overprotect or possess us.

This shows a temporary emotional or sexual difficulty. If we are involved in a rela-tionship, then we need our own space yet feel somewhat isolated from our partner or unable to communicate our anxieties. Often a separate career, regular time away from home, or a separate room in the house as a study would work wonders. Sometimes when we don't get the freedom we crave (or we feel par-ticularly fenced in), we may look elsewhere and begin a secret sex life or relationship – we will look for an affair without the domestic routine attached to married life.

Please note that this is not a guarantee, by any means, that someone who has their little finger away from the ring finger will be unfaithful. The need for freedom and independence in relationships is what characterises this finger position.

Actress Katharine Hepburn (herself a palmist) once said that men and women should live next door and visit occasionally – that sentiment could well fit those of us with this position. If this position is not temporary but the little finger always stays jutted out, then our partner needs to be aware that we need a day off every now and again, and that we need to avoid restrictive, suffocating unions. When this finger juts out, we who are single are not ready for an intense, 24-hour-a-day relationship. We prefer to remain footloose or seek relationships with no strings attached. Perhaps recent hurts are still at the forefront of our mind. When the finger returns closer to the hand, we are willing to share and trust more easily.

k. Little finger significantly lower-set than other fingers

This feature is remarkably frequent these days, and reveals a parental fixation due to a feeling of loss or misunderstanding with one parent. It is unlikely to alter position except in childhood.

I've found this position to be most relevant when one parent (usually the father) is emotionally or physically absent during childhood. There is need for compen-sation, and there can be a quest for a psychological understanding of this parent (and the parental relationship). If the parent is still alive, communication may be the best means to reach a level of understanding. Until this has been reached, we may find ourselves attracted to partners who are either very similar to or the extreme opposite of the parent in question. (For example, the woman who wakes up one day to realise that she is married to her father and has become her mother.) Often we compare our partner unfairly to a parent (for good or ill), which

The relative positions of the fingers and thumbs change as circumstances change. The hands of Princess Diana were fascinating to observe. At the start of her marriage she held her thumb very close into her hand (a), suggesting her reticence in accepting her role on the world stage. Later the thumb moved outwards from the palm (b) when her confidence grew, the little finger protruded (j), signalling her partnership difficulties and need for space, and her ring and middle fingers moved closer together (f). The latter betrayed her inhibition and sense of guilt, and perhaps the strictures imposed upon her by her public role and others' expectations. In addition, the index finger (which was naturally long, indicating her innate femininity and need to direct her own life) was held out away from the others (d), marking her need to assert herself in her surroundings.

may leave them competing with our impossibly high standards. What is perhaps needed is for us to find a partner whose temperament is a balance between these extremes. Understanding the parent's motivations or character will help us find this balance. It's important to identify the relationship roles we assume and change any destructive patterns.

Q: Looking at Palm Print 22, who is the more held in, reserved and conservative with others, Palm A or B?

In Palm A the fingers are all spread out, which indicates someone who hates to be tied down or restricted. The hand looks open and receptive, as though they want others to know how generous they are with their time, energy and money. They are unable to accept the confines of everyday 9 to 5 work or the constraints of a suffocating relationship. The need for freedom is paramount and they may be considered anti-social because they refuse to be a regular member of a group. They need freedom and space to explore life and their personalities.

Palm B belongs to someone who is a conformist and conservative in her approach to life. Look how the fingers are held together – this reveals reticence and self-restraint. People with hands held like Palm B fear spontaneous movement, preferring the safety of observing but doing nothing. They are cautious and can be insecure, inhibited and uptight. They are introverted and can be acutely introspective. At work, they are methodical, tackle projects thoroughly and keep their cards close to their chests. John Major, the former British Prime Minister, is one example of a shy personality whose fingers are held

Palm Print 22
Reserved and outgoing palms

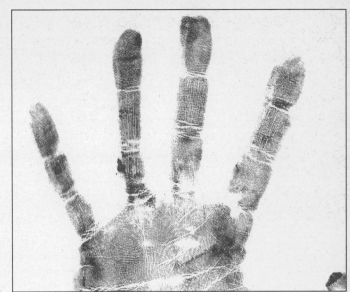

Palm A

Palm B

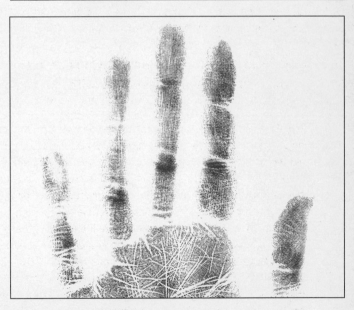

together. Astrologically, it is not uncommon to find Capricorn or the planet Saturn emphasised in the horoscope of people with this kind of palm. In Major's birth chart both the Moon and Ascendant are found in Capricorn.

Step 4
Finger Print Patterns

Our Psychological Blueprint

Our finger prints are our genetic markers, our inherited characteristics and attitudes. Together with the hand shape they represent the most basic aspects of our personality. Finger prints, like the relative length of fingers, are determined in the womb, appearing on the hands by the fifth month of foetal development, and are the unchangeable foundations of our inherited character. The finger prints reflect a unique record of what was happening in the womb during pregnancy. They are permanent and unique. Scientists don't know why the finger prints form patterns, but hand analysts recognise their importance in identifying genetic personality traits. Hand analyst Lori Reid calls them vividly, 'the visible signature of the DNA' and 'infallible indicators of all your personal ambitions, skills, and even your interests'.

Dermatoglyphics

Dermatoglyphics is the scientific name for the skin (papillary) ridges that form weaving patterns all over the palm. These ridges form loops, whorls and apices (triangular meeting points) over the palm surface. These markings can be significant – for example, the Memory Loop, shown in Palm Print 23, indicates an excellent memory prompted by emotional recollections. We will look further at the significance of some of these features in Part 3, 'Love, Health and Career'.

The Finger Print Types

There are three basic finger print patterns, the loop, the whorl, and the arch, as shown in Palm Print 24, along with several variations on these three patterns. Loops appear on approximately 65% of all prints, arches 5–6%, and whorls on 30%, although these statistics vary across races. For example, loops are more common in Anglo-Saxons, whilst whorls appear with greater regularity in the hands of Germans and Danes.

To view finger prints clearly and determine which category each falls into, it is better to read them from a print made by ink, lipstick or powder. Examine all ten prints. You will find that most of us have two or more types. Count them all to determine the most important type on the hand, but *take into account that the thumb and index finger prints on both hands are the most important* in confirming character deductions made from other aspects in the hand.

The three basic patterns of finger prints and some other variations are shown in Palm Print 24. For further information read *The Science at Your Fingertips Educational Series* by Joseph M. Ludas.

Palm Print 23
The Memory Loop

Palm Print 24 Examples of finger print types

Three basic patterns:

LOOP
resembles a delta lake
or U-Turn

WHORL
resembles a circle or
target

Other formations of these patterns:

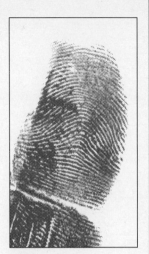

ARCH
resembles a hill

TENTED ARCH
resembles a camping
tent

COMPOSITE
a type of accidental
whorl with two separate
loop formations

PEACOCK'S EYE
a type of whorl with a
central loop pocket

LOOP ARCH
the loop and arch share
the print equally

Loop

The loop indicates a versatile, adaptable nature. Loops are found on easy-going people who are able to get along with others. When loops appear on most or all of the fingers, indecisiveness often creeps in.

We are the salesmen, the retail assistants, and the chatty, nervous types who always have time to gossip and discuss everyday matters and other people's business. We seek variety and are endlessly curious, particularly about other people. We are the ones who love to follow dramas on television and the continuous trials and tribulations of characters in soap operas. We usually have active lifestyles, many friends and high telephone bills! The loop can imply that we are lightweights, perhaps too shallow at times, and rarely rock the boat. To protect our health – particularly from nervous tension or fatigue – we need rest, solitude and down time without commitments, dates and events on our social calendars.

Often loops are found high on the finger tip, which suggests a greater sensitivity (more attuned to the element of Water) and higher ideals. Loops can travel from the direction of the little finger towards the thumb or from the thumb outwards.

Whorl

The whorl marks its owner with a distinctive temperament or talent. Whorl-dominated hands are found on intense people who are individual in manner and in everything they set out to do – from their dress sense to their approach to creative work. Often only the ring finger will house a whorl, and here we find a talent for art, architecture, design or music. Sooner or later, whorls tend to show themselves productively in their owner's life.

With whorls we are offbeat, dramatic and usually self-obsessed. Having many whorls certainly marks us out as unusual, unique individuals unable to conform. We are people of extremes, from our tastes to our reactions. We are intensely single-minded, goal-orientated and need to get the very most out of life. We hate to lose and are often disagreeable or deliberately provocative, contrary or perverse in the face of opposition or ridicule. We need time to process information and have tremendous powers of concentration. Others should not mistake this for indecisiveness and should be wary of interrupting us when we're highly focused on work matters. We look to the future and often have the gift of insight into what may be popular or fashionable in the future.

Strangely, there's often a lack of family around; friends are sporadic and we often feel as though we should be in another country. We can feel alien and sometimes isolated. Being secretive, we keep some past experiences locked away and never reveal these to anyone. We should release pent-up emotional feelings. Studies (as reported in the *British Medical Journal*, 14 August 1993, pp. 405–409) show that people with whorls, particularly on the right hand, have raised blood pressure in adult life. Additional studies have related right hand whorls to hypertension.

All the people I have met with a whorl on at least 7 or 8 digits have been quite exceptional and have had unusual, marketable skills. They have been different from the norm in their style of dress, attitudes or physical behaviour. And they act like a law unto themselves, making their own life rules. One client was a misogynist who alienated all the women around her; one was a noted eccentric with bizarre hair and clothes; another client had an incapacitating stutter that drew attention to her. Although I never had the chance to meet him, one can speculate that the eccentric writer Quentin Crisp carried many whorls on his finger tips.

Arch

An arch demonstrates an efficient, practical personality. People with arches often veer towards skilled manual work because they need to be productive and to learn a trade. Many of my clients with arches have worked in mechanics, engineering, ceramics or sculpture. Many can apply themselves to any outdoor or physical pursuit, too. There's an earthiness about them, so gardening and nature can provide the right outlet. They may have an aversion to modern technology because it is less hands-on than they would like.

With an arch on a finger we need to be down-to-earth in the area governed by that finger – we want others to see us as ordinary, approachable and unpretentious. Arches are found most commonly on the index finger, suggesting a no-nonsense, practical nature and attitude to life. For those of us willing to experience new challenges, energy healing and Reiki would be an interesting way of expressing the hands-on character of this finger pattern. At home we like to rule the roost with a firm hand, often learning a great deal about discipline – or lack of it – from our own childhood. We can be surprisingly shy, often have low self-esteem and develop a tough, resistant exterior or – if we have loops on other fingers – play the clown to off-set criticism or ridicule. We question the motives of others and at times mistrust our own instincts. At work we are results-driven and effective, although somewhat self-protective and anti-social. We persevere until we achieve our aims – realising nothing comes without hard work and dedication – and we wear down obstacles with stubborn resistance. We encounter more difficulties than most, so we need to learn about business to become self-reliant and must find a way to articulate our emotions. One music client wrote, recorded and performed a set of songs to vent his anger over his partner's betrayal; he said it was the best therapy he could have had.

Tented arch

The key to this print is contagious enthusiasm, making those with it able to inspire others. The tented arch is often found only on the index finger.

We show a marked interest in pursuing new projects and get fired up making plans for the future. Unfortunately our interest can wane (a fresher, newer and more exciting challenge undoubtedly arises) and we can be labelled as ideas people who don't follow through. We have an insatiable curiosity and often turn our hands to teaching, research work or fighting for a cause or an injustice. We are great motivators and inspirational lecturers, with a strong interest in cutting-edge material. We also have a great interest in other people and their lives, so biographies and biopics hold our attention.

Composite

Usually found only on the thumb and index finger, this is a sign of indecision and an ability to see both sides of a situation.

To others we can appear souls in torment because we often face dilemmas, feel torn between needs and responsibilities, or are perpetually in the process of making big, life-changing decisions. We must learn to trust our intuition more. We can, however, offer others the benefit of our experience and analysis, making good strategists and therapists. We are good mediators and magistrates, and our diplomatic nature helps us get what we want from others. We are able to see all sides and weigh up the pros and cons of an important course of action...unless it involves our own personal matters. Then we can appear to procrastinate endlessly, even if we are only choosing an outfit for a party!

Peacock's eye

This is an unusual print. When found it is usually only on the ring or little fingers. General consensus suggests this print is associated with lucky people who feel protected in some way.

Many of my clients who have this print have spoken of the belief that an angel protects and looks over them, particularly in times of danger (accidents, for example). While some have a fascination with angels, others believe that a deceased relative watches over and guides them.

Loop arch

This is a combination of the arch and the loop prints, where both prints share the finger tip equally. It is frequently found. It reflects a possible Jack of all Trades because there's so much these people want to accomplish.

We are versatile and skilled but have great trouble settling down. Others may see us as a perpetual student or someone who never grew up. In some ways we share the restlessness of those with a tented arch because our versatile nature is always interested in the next thing, and we can leave work unfinished.

We need proper training and are advised to specialise in one area before moving on to another.

SYNTHESIS PART 8:
FINGER PRINT MIX AND MATCH

The meaning of each finger print can be matched to the symbolism of the finger, as indicated below.

Thumb print: our temperament and method of applying our energy
Index finger print: our temperament and method of self-assertion
Middle finger print: our attitude to work and responsibilities
Ring finger print: our creative aptitudes
Little finger print: our type of communication and sexual attitudes

Here are some examples:
- A loop on the thumb would reveal a flexible approach to tasks
- A loop on the middle finger needs a job working with others
- A whorl on the thumb demonstrates a stubborn refusal to do things anybody else's way and a forcefulness in expressing innovative ideas
- A whorl on the index finger suggests a truth-seeker who is also highly self-involved
- A whorl on the middle finger suggests a need to be a specialist, and there is often a marked change from one set path to another
- A whorl on the ring finger indicates a sense of drama, artistic creativity and a prima donna attitude
- A whorl on the little finger reveals an intense way of communicating (and often, inventive sex games)

Other Quick Steps to Determine Character Traits

Rings

We can understand current mental worries and preoccupations by noting which fingers bear rings. These will reveal matters that are foremost in our minds and the personality traits we wish to emphasise. (See page 73 for lists of character-istics.) Of course, wearing a ring does not cause any of these circumstances or traits. It is simply that *the desire to wear a ring reflects and coincides with a current problem or urgent need,* as revealed by the finger in question. In addition, the size of the ring adds emphasis to the particular meaning. A very large ring would reveal that the matter had become quite an obsession.

Thumb

A ring on the thumb shows a wilful, stubborn temperament; we can be hell-bent on doing things our own way regardless of outside influence or suggestion. We like to control our environment. If worn on the left hand it will show that this need for autonomy is dogmatically applied to our personal life; on the right hand it is inflicted upon co-workers and in the pursuit of professional projects.

Index finger

A ring on the index finger indicates that we need to exhibit traits of leadership and confidence, although hiding shyness or protecting a fragile ego may be the underlying motive. When the index finger is longer than the ring finger, the wearing of a ring can highlight the control freak in us or suggest that we want to impose our authority on others. If the ring is worn on the left hand, we may play the role of the bossy homemaker with the henpecked spouse; on the right hand it shows that we want to be firmly in control of our destiny.

Middle and ring fingers

I wouldn't say that a ring on the middle finger is particularly significant (although some palmists suggest it reflects a fear of loneliness), nor is the wearing of a ring on the ring finger (although as a sign of romantic commitment it emphasises the astrological qualities of Venus and the Sun).

Little finger

Have you ever noticed how top businessmen wear rings on their little fingers? Like the finger itself, a ring worn here has multiple interpretations. On the left hand we may be living through temporary sexual or romantic problems. We have a need for freedom in a personal relationship (more importantly, this will be shown when the little finger juts out away from the rest of the fingers). At times, money takes over as the prime motivator in getting romantically involved (the gold-digger may wear rings on both little fingers). Sometimes there are sexual difficulties or physical worries – we feel inadequate in the bedroom. This latter point will be backed up by other features, which we shall discover later.

I've always remembered the particularly vivid example of a client who revealed that for the whole time she wore a ring on her left hand little finger she was also experiencing an on-going gynaecological problem. After her hysterectomy she took the ring off, declaring it 'no longer felt right on my hand'. This is an extreme case, but I've found the wearing of a ring on the little finger to highlight anxieties or physical problems time and time again.

When the ring is worn on the right hand, the emphasis is more on acquisition. Money-makers, people obsessed with financial gain, and avaricious types often wear a ring on their right little finger. The larger the ring, the greater the obsession with the almighty dollar.

Finger Tip Shapes
Pointed

We are sensitive and impressionable. This is a feminine sign suggesting receptivity and a psychic awareness of mood and feeling, as well as a need to control matters. On the index finger this may indicate a psychic talent or simply an instinct to nag or boss others around. On the little finger we can charm the birds from the trees with our silver tongue.

Rounded

This is the most common for finger tips, showing a well-rounded approach to life and an adaptable nature. This can, however, be off-set by numerous other factors in the hands.

Square

A need for structure, reasoning and order is inherent with square-ish tips. Others should be aware of our tidiness, punctuality and an industrious, almost pedantic, approach to work – particularly when square tips are found on our index or middle fingers.

Spatulate

The strongest feature of this type is a need for freedom in everyday matters – sportspeople and those who work outdoors usually have spatulate fingers. We are energetic and restless, loving physical activity, usually outdoors. Often we are adventurers, eager to climb mountains or try risky sports for the sheer thrill of participation, and we thrive when having to meet deadlines. Feeling a rush of adrenaline is a strong motivating factor, and we will avoid partners who are wet blankets and afraid to explore or travel with us.

Spatulate tips are most commonly found on the ring finger, and this shows an ability to work with the public. We are prima donnas and can express our ideas in a dramatic manner. Spatulate tips on the index finger show we have a sense of adventure, a need for freedom and often appear sure of our abilities. This tip is found on the middle finger of those of us for whom work cannot be a regular 9 to 5 job.

Nails

Just as we pick up and manipulate objects with our fingers, nails are our tools to scratch away at objects, to pick at or clean things. When we are nervously

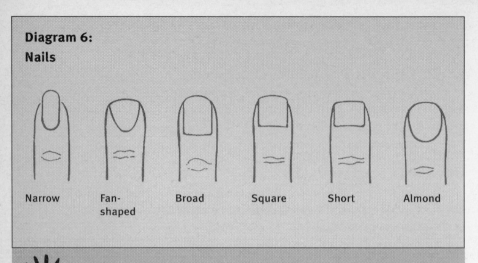

**Diagram 6:
Nails**

Narrow   Fan-   Broad   Square   Short   Almond
          shaped

Did you know that nails register upsets, shocks and other traumas? Nails on healthy adult hands take between four and six months to grow from the cuticle to the tip. A trauma that occurred three months ago would appear as a slight ridge bent at about halfway up the nail from the cuticle.

awaiting news or are anxious about an outcome we bite or pick our nails. Thus nails are, in effect, indicators of how we assess, analyse, pick at and take apart situations. The significance of the different nail shapes, shown in Diagram 6, is described below. To understand this more fully, look at the fingers they appear on and link the nail with the area ruled by the finger. Watch out for the shape having been manicured away! Only look at the area covering the nail bed.

Narrow and fan-shaped nails

These two types reveal single-mindedness, but our approach is often to assess matters and people in a narrow-minded and conservative fashion. We may not be willing to take on board new ideas or situations. At worst we can pigeonhole people from past observations – or prejudice – in one fell swoop.

Broad nails

Broad nails show broad-mindedness and openness to new experiences. We try to assess ideas and people fairly, leaving the door open for change, improvement and our own fallibility when making assessments. At times we need to be more discriminating and show better judgement. When our nails are naturally short and broad we add a dynamic, sometimes aggressive thrust to proceedings, relying on impulsive assessments rather than listening to reason.

Square nails

Square nails reveal an orderly approach to ideas and people. We assess matters carefully in a methodical manner. At worst we forget to allow for differences and exceptions to the rule, and let dogmatism into our assessments.

Short nails

These show that we are quick judges of people and situations, but we can lack patience and tire easily of those who don't live up to our expectations or conform to our rigid moral standards. At worst we can jump to conclusions, enjoy playing devil's advocate and tear apart new ideas with strong criticism.

Almond-shaped nails

Almond-shaped nails point to an insular approach to new matters, basing every assessment on our own limited – and often materialistic – sphere of reference. Our analytical abilities need to be sharpened up and we would benefit from a greater sense of discernment.

Other Hand Features

The colour, texture and malleability of the palms and fingers should also be considered.

Colour

According to Lori Reid the colour of the hand can reflect both temperament and the general state of health: palms that are too red are a sign of high blood pressure, pugnacity, energy and liver problems. If our hands are very red we should consider ways of releasing aggression and anger through a sporting activity. Very white palms reveal a lack of warmth, poor circulation and low energy. Blue-ish palms expose circulatory or respiratory problems, and yellow palms reveal jaundice, hepatitis or high cholesterol.

Texture

The texture of the hand provides an early clue to the person's nature, but don't forget to take into consideration the age of the person as well as the sort of work they do – both can have an influence. Coarse hands can show that we are tough survivors, while soft hands show sensitivity. If you are looking for extra tenderness or refinement you should pursue those with softer hands. Although soft hands demonstrate sensitivity, if they are also flabby, this points to a need for pampering, a love of luxury and a hedonistic approach to life. At worst we can be lazy and self-indulgent.

Malleability

Firm hands show resilience and backbone. Stiff hands reveal stubbornness, pent up frustration and an inability to change. Great suppleness is a sign that we are flexible but can be easily influenced. We must form our own opinions and lead an independent life, and not let family or partners make decisions for us. When the fingers – particularly the finger tips – are very flexible (i.e. they can be bent backwards) this reveals an extroverted, people person, and a lack of discipline with money. Firm fingers and finger tips show an unyielding temperament – we have a strong sense of right or wrong and can be inflexible in our attitudes.

QUICK QUIZ 3

1. What is the key sign of a strong character?

2. Which finger is a measure of our confidence and self-esteem?

3. Which feature is common in those who are ingenuous or immature in relationships?

4. Which phalange governs our business sense and ability to organise our finances?

5. Which digit stands out when we are feeling at ease and open with others?

6. Which feature is found on those who would feel guilty for enjoying life to the full?

7. Which finger print pattern reveals a practical but shy character?

8. Talented, provocative and stubborn types are likely to have which finger print type?

9. A creative nature or artistic talent is likely to be seen by which print on which finger tip?

10. Enthusiasm and an inspirational way to teach new ideas would be shown by which print on which finger tip?

(Answers in Appendix 3, page 218.)

Part 2

TIMING TECHNIQUES

By examining the hand we tap into the life we're living *at present*. The future that can be seen on the hand is where we are currently heading because of the choices we have made and are making *right now*, and is not a fixed, inescapable path that we're doomed to walk down regardless of personal freedom or will. We can always make different choices. We need to take responsibility for our thoughts and actions, as the truth is that we achieve what we expect to achieve and we create our own reality.

This section can be used as a tool to help us get on the right track, see events in perspective and live in the moment. Lines show our present circumstances and the path we have taken to reach where we are today. A good palmist will look at the hand shape, fingers, major lines and finger prints to become acquainted with character motivations and needs, and then be able to understand reactions to past events and anticipate the responses to forthcoming life challenges. We can then see future indications in the hand as opportunities to be aware of possible pitfalls and make better choices. If future strain is indicated in the hand, we need to be aware of the reasons why it may develop. Being in control of our journey is far more important than anticipating every turn.

Timing Events

Timing events on the hand takes a great deal of practice. When reading the future from the Fate Line, for example, it is wise to look at the corresponding times on the other major lines to confirm the timing of and reactions to possible future events. When checking past events, while it is important to know what actually happened, it is more important to note the *reaction* to the event. To demonstrate this, the profiles in *Palmistry 4 Today* contain details of past events.

Whatever the event shown in the hand, remember to look first at the character of the person. This will show what motivates them and how they will respond to events.

Diagram 7 shows the timings on the four most reliable lines to time on our hands: the Life Line, the Fate Line, the Apollo Line and the Head Line. You may wonder why on the Fate Line, for example, so much space on the hand is given to the period from 21 to 35. This is because it is during this time that we make major decisions that can affect the course of the rest of our life. 35 is an important crossroads and is usually shown by the intersection of the Head and Fate lines. More people are now changing direction in their 40s, 50s and 60s, but the early years are key times when we first encounter love, work and responsibility. Gail Sheehy in *New Passages* has coined the phrase the 'Tryout Twenties' for this period (the prolonged adolescence during which we take chances and

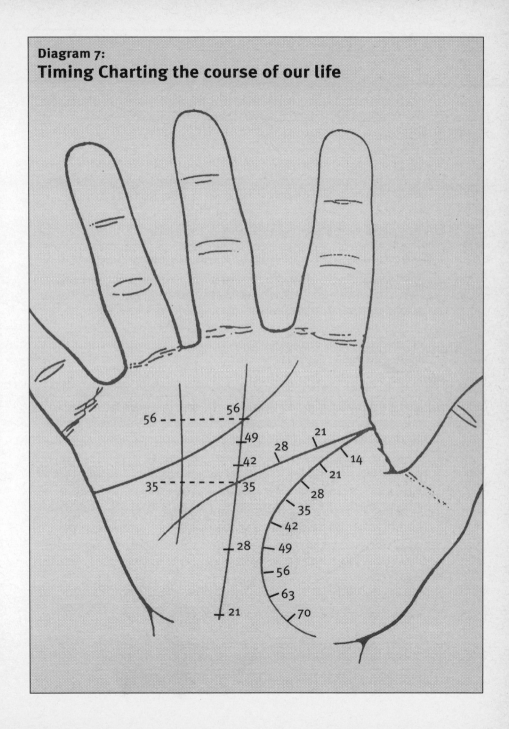

Diagram 7:
Timing Charting the course of our life

Time on our hands...some tips

• The most reliable lines to time on our hands are the Life Line, the Fate Line, the Apollo Line (see page 191) and the Head Line. The crossing lines, breaks, islands and other markings on these important lines can all be timed from the position at whichthey intersect or join the line.

• Timing the Heart Line and the Relationship Lines above this line are not easy, and existing methods can be unreliable. This may be because pinpointing times when the heart begins or stops feeling an emotional response is often impossible. These lines can give a general overview of the emotional course of events, but relationships can be timed more accurately on other lines.

• As with character analysis, it's important to synthesise many different aspects when timing the hand. Don't make assessments from one marking only, but use the Three Principle: we should see a particular characteristic or important event register on the palm in three separate ways. A life-changing event is likely to show up on the Life Line (a change of physical – perhaps geographic – circumstance), on the Fate Line (a change in life path) and probably also on the Head Line (a change in attitude).

• When examining a marking on a line, check to see if the line improves or weakens after this particular mark. This will be a clear indication of whether the marking is of a positive nature or not. For example, if a period of mental frustration, stress or breakdown (as sometimes shown by an island in the Head Line) is followed by a stronger Head Line, this would be a beneficial sign, suggesting the person will get themselves together and feel a lot stronger mentally and emotionally. I saw this a few years ago on the Head Line of a man who had desperate financial troubles and was always looking for the easy way out. After the threat of prison for theft and the prospect of not seeing his two children he put his life back on track. If, however, the hand signals a more difficult time ahead (with depression lines or a feathery Head Line) we should see this as an opportunity to recognise potential problems and to take advantage of this knowledge to strengthen our Head Line by firming up our ideas and willpower. We may have failed in some way, but we need to pick ourselves up and move on.

• It's important not to be put off by difficult future markings in the hand. If we have knowledge of what the future may hold, this can be turned into a learning experience and/or an opportunity to see how we can change our lives.

attempt to fulfil dreams). This in turn leads to the 'Turbulent Thirties' (the 'serious dress rehearsal' as we prepare for future leadership positions – a period of new ambitions, decisions and juggling numerous time-demanding roles). As we get older, the years fly by quicker, and this is shown by the disparity in the lines on the hand. On the Life Line I rarely time the pre-teen years or look beyond the age of 65. At these important times the overall impression of the hands (the lines, finger prints and hand shape) reveals far more information than does examining the minute detail in the hand.

Timing Life Changes on the Hand

Before looking in detail at timing on each of the individual lines, let's take a closer look at the most important signs and markings found on the lines. Remember that the crossing lines, breaks, islands and other markings on these important lines can all be timed from the position at which they intersect or join the line. Remember to consider whether the line in question improves or worsens after the markings.

Sudden stops, gaps and overlaps

When a line stops abruptly, there's an ending of a chapter. When there's a noticeable gap in a line, a rest is called for because of recent upheavals. Often an event has caught us by surprise but it should not discourage us in the long term. We need to dust ourselves off, get up and begin again – even if we are afraid of travelling uncharted waters. Overlaps show that we must react to a recent event by making a planned change in our life. Timing stops, gaps and overlaps can be tricky because there's usually a period of adjustment, but the main physical shift occurs at the stage when the new line becomes the dominant one.
In the following descriptions the letters refer to the features shown in Diagram 8.

a. The Life Line stops suddenly
We need to take stock of our recent lifestyle and choices. If an illness has led us to this point, we need to reassess the path we are on. If the line is fainter when it continues after the stop, we must make extra effort to keep involved in the world around us rather than allow ourselves to be put off by recent obstacles.

b. The Head Line stops suddenly
It's time to be more flexible, consider other work possibilities and approach personal problems from a different angle. If people cause trouble, examine difficulties from the other person's perspective, consider possibilities for

Diagram 8:
Stops, gaps and overlaps on the major lines

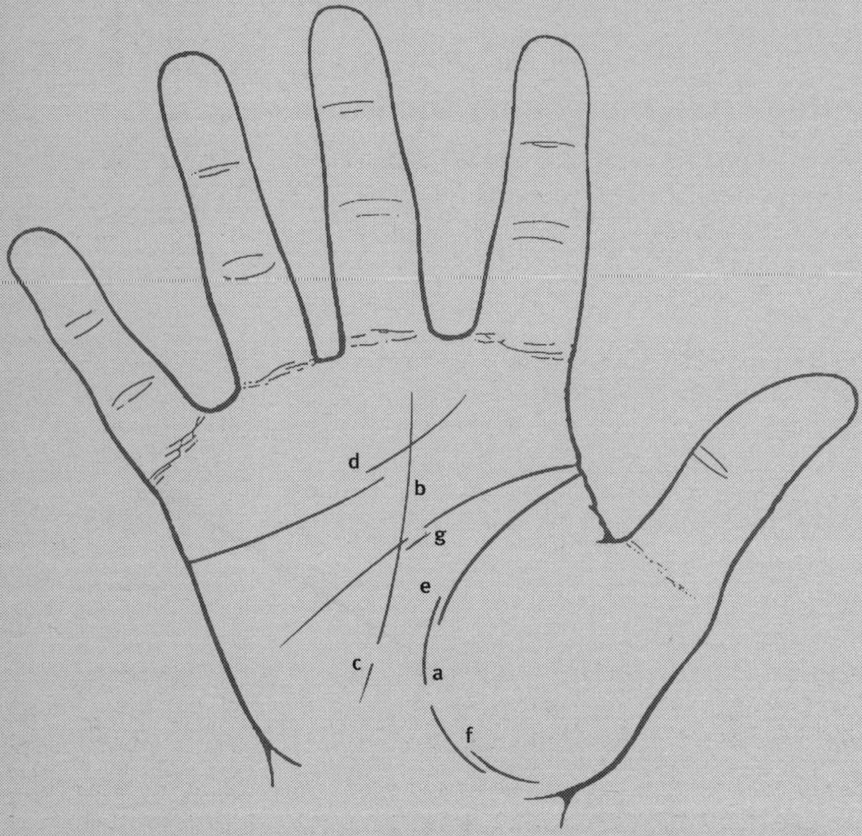

reconciliation or move on. Think positively and don't look back.

Often there may be a faint line under the break (**g**). This acts as a support during the transition.

c. The Fate Line stops suddenly

This is our warning either to patch up recent problems or to have the courage to make a clean break. At times we may be forced to rest, for example by an unexpected pregnancy or unemployment. At other times this signifies our decision to change priorities and spend our life in a less regimented daily routine.

When the Fate Line ends and appears to be replaced by the Apollo Line we can expect fortune to smile on us because of our own efforts to find happiness. Our life seems less of a struggle and we have time to pursue creative paths and hobbies, or enjoy parenthood or playing the proud grandparent. (See Palm Profile 1 on page 114 for an example of how dramatic changes in lifestyle are shown in the Fate Line.)

d. The Heart Line has a noticeable break

This can show the hurt felt from a relationship that has come to an end. With this marking we may nurse a broken heart or feel a sense of longing for the past. The presence of Heartbreak Lines (see page 150) on the Mount of Venus would confirm this. We must consider seeking professional advice for recent health or relationship upsets. If we have suffered a trauma or heartbreak we should keep friends close by.

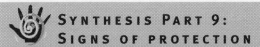

SYNTHESIS PART 9: SIGNS OF PROTECTION

Where there is an overlap on a line, check to see if there is a square present around the overlap. This is a sign that times are challenging but that we are able to move forward from the rocky period with a better understanding of the situation. As the lines overlap, we can expect the change to be a gradual one. Even if circumstances end abruptly, with an overlap, we take time to shift gear. Often squares last many years, so we must learn to be flexible, roll with the punches and remain firm in our belief that this too will pass.

e. and f. Overlapping Life Lines

These signify that we should consider changing our diet, lifestyle or surroundings.

If the new, lower line is further into the palm (e) circumstances encourage (or force) us to become more involved in the world. These are times when we discover more confidence or find work, friends or a hobby that pushes us out to meet new people and develop and understand ourselves. They can also show times of travel to new places. The higher up in the hand, the earlier in the life it occurs. With strong overlapping Life Lines we have the capacity to change our lives completely, whether it is our job, marriage or any current major circumstance.

If the new Life Line begins inside the Life Line, near the thumb (f), our health may force us to be more isolated. Perhaps we become scared of life and people. We should fight an instinct to hide away and make efforts to become more involved in the world. It's common for this line to occur at the end of the Life Line, towards the wrist. At this age the doctor may advise us to slow down, spend more time at home or enjoy our retirement. We all need to be aware that our bodies may slow down as we get older, but to slow down mentally is to invite early death. To stop work completely at 60 or 65 is a mistake – the body and mind both receive a shock. When this overlap is present in our hands, we must keep busy, discover new adventures, fight boredom and seek challenge.

Examples of overlaps on the Head and Fate Lines are shown in Palm Prints 25 and 26.

Palm Print 25
Overlapping Head Lines

It's time for a new approach to our life. Perhaps we have recently been 'born again', divorced, introduced to a life-changing course or undergone a spiritual rebirth. We need to reassess our position, give up the past and embrace our new mental attitude. Interestingly, this can be the sign of a past head injury, where there has been a long recuperation period and a new approach to life. In this print this occurs between the ages of 30 and 31.

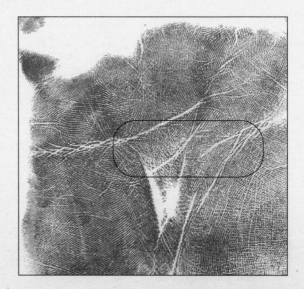

Palm Print 26

Overlapping Fate Lines

Although circumstances may seem insurmountable, we can make a smooth transition if we realise that a change of life path is necessary. Often this overlap is a signpost heralding a forthcoming marriage or parental responsibility. In this print this occurs between the ages of 32 and 34.

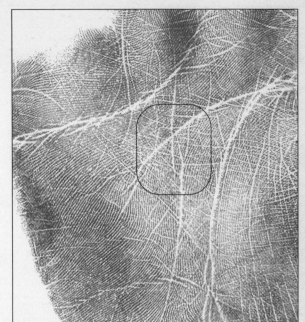

Palm Print 27

Overlapping Life Lines protected by a series of squares

This is the print of a woman who moved out of home at 15, after the death of her father, to start an independent life as a performer and musician. There were troubles ahead, most notably a botched abortion at 18 that almost killed her. At 24 she left the music profession, she became a mother, went through tough financial times and found religion at 26.

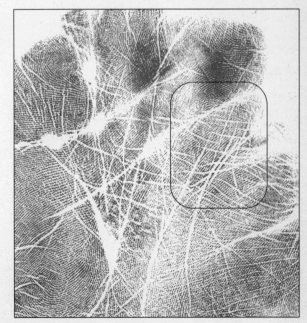

Fay Presto

This is the palm print of magician Fay Presto, who went through a dramatic change of lifestyle in her early 30s, during which she says, 'I rendered myself unemployable.' Note how the Fate Line has two distinct gaps and begins again at the age of 31 (with a strong secondary line rising from the Life Line indicating a personal effort to start over or change lifestyle). This was the period when Fay completed a series of operations and began a new life as a woman. Looking for a profession that could accommodate her, Fay rejected beauty therapy, theatre and fashion for the applause and showmanship of a life in magic, which she began at 35. The Fate Line shifts slightly when it meets the Head Line at 35, and the emergence of two branch lines to the ring finger at 33 and 34 from the Fate Line points to self-realisation and inner contentment from life choices (as shown by the Fate Line). She developed her craft, reputation and high-profile client base, which now includes celebrities and royalty. Other features include a strong thumb held close to the hand, indicating a bloody-minded, stubborn individual who is also self-protective and essentially a private person. With the Loop of Seriousness (pages 185 and 190) showing dedication to her craft, and a square palm, she has a strong moral code and maintains personal integrity. With a curved Head Line and Humanitarian Heart Line (page 151) she is 'not a planner or strategist. I shoot from the hip and usually hit target', directing her forceful nature and sense of justice towards campaigning for others who are victims of what she describes as a 'joke' and 'genetic mistake'.

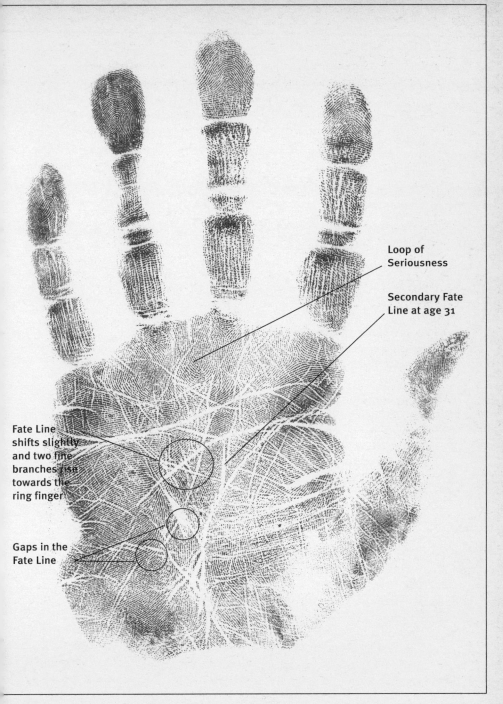

Loop of
Seriousness

Secondary Fate
Line at age 31

Fate Line
shifts slightly
and two fine
branches rise
towards the
ring finger

Gaps in the
Fate Line

Branch lines

Branch lines are timed according to the exact position at which they connect to the major line. These are lines of effort, ambition or achievement. They are always short, hair lines and have a two-fold application, showing the times when we make effort to change our circumstances and also revealing an innate character trait. To be branch lines they must rise from the line itself, not from another point. Note which finger the line is directed towards and use your knowledge of the individual meanings of fingers to establish in which area the effort is focused.

In the following descriptions the letters refer to the features shown in Diagram 9.

a. From Life Line up towards middle finger

Branch lines rising towards the middle finger reveal periods in life when we must make large investments of time and/or money, for example, financing or raising money to start a new business, home or partnership. Don't mistake these for longer and deeper lines rising from the Life Line to the middle finger, which are in fact Fate Lines suggesting a late surge of effort to achieve. The latter are signs of the self-made person (see pages 130 and 165 (bottom) for examples).
Character traits: responsible, committed.

b. From Life Line up towards little finger

Lines rising in this direction are rare and usually begin lower down on the Life Line. They indicate efforts to improve finances or times of greater financial reward. More common are lines rising from the Head Line towards the little finger, which have the same meaning.
Character traits: financially astute.

c. From Life Line down towards the outer edge of the hand

This shows times of travel, moving to a new location or, when the Life Line remains stronger than the branch line, periods when we desire to move.
Character traits: restless.

d. From Life Line but curled inwards towards the thumb

Possibly a difficult time, when we consider withdrawing from our work because of health worries.
Character traits: fearful.

Diagram 9:
Branch lines

e. From Head Line towards index finger or vice versa

This shows a renewed belief in ourselves, a time of greater confidence or a special achievement (for example, a book being published).
Character traits: articulate or confident.

f. From Head Line towards little finger

We are looking for financial reward and to be paid our due. Note this branch should turn up towards the little finger, otherwise it could be classified as a Writer's Fork (page 196).
Character traits: materialistic.

g. From Head Line towards middle finger or vice versa

This indicates a time of growing financial, family or business responsibilities. See example on page 130.

Character traits: authoritative; science- or business-minded.

Other branch lines:

• From Life Line up towards index finger

Lines rising from the Life Line are often known as Ambition Lines. Where there are many of these rising from the Life Line (regardless of direction) it shows that we naturally want to improve ourselves and our circumstances – this is the sign of the high achiever and the restless person (see Palm Print 28).

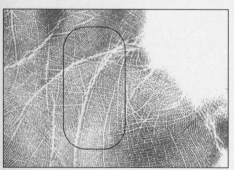

Rising lines to the index finger point to a need for independence. They occur at the age we left home, branched out or made some effort towards a new goal or career. Earlier on they show academic achievement, later they show the first push into 'real life' as an adult, and later still they can reveal times of great achievement and the fulfilment of long-held ambitions. They act as excellent motivators, for they foretell times when we can still make an impact and be proud of our individual contribu-

Palm Print 28

Many Ambition Lines rising from the Life Line

tion. (Don't mistake this type of branch line for a Life Line that begins under the index finger; this will be a stronger line and a sign of great enthusiasm and ambition in life as a youngster.)

Character traits: freedom-seeking, independent.

• From Life Line up towards ring finger

Lines rising in this direction indicate times of personal fulfilment or creative accomplishment. (You'll see one on the hand of Cleo Laine, page 204). A few celebrities who became well-known as children or teenagers have lines rising early in the Life Line towards the ring finger, signalling their early brush with fame and the opportunities this opened up for them. Don't mistake this for a Relationship Line, which starts from within the Life Line (see page 136).

Character traits: creatively productive.

• From Head Line towards ring finger

This represents a time when the extra effort we have made to pursue creative ventures results in a sense of personal fulfilment and some measure of professional acknowledgement and kudos. See also the example of Catherine on page 124.

Character traits: talented and artistic.

Islands

Islands represent periods of restriction. They can appear on any of the lines and they chart difficult times in our lives. Their presence on a particular line can also reveal a physical weakness.

a. Island early on Life Line

This signals early problems in life, feeling trapped, misunderstood by family or teachers, periods of ill-health or physical restriction. In the days when illegitimacy was frowned upon, it could reveal a mystery about the birth, particularly the identity of the father.

b. Island later on Life Line

When this appears we need to break free from our surroundings. Sometimes it accompanies a period of ill-health or physical weakness. The problem can continue until the island closes (see 'Timing on the Life Line', page 121). Its presence shows that we are looking for a way out of our present conditions or circumstances. When it appears later in the Life Line it shows a possible prolonged period of ill-health that should be avoided. It is important to time the island and avoid falling prey to illness at this time.

An interesting example can be found in the hand of palmist Andrew Fitzherbert, who was sentenced to life imprisonment on 2 August 1999 for a brutal murder. Information from the palms alone cannot determine innocence or guilt. What can be seen, however, are the personal repercussions of an involvement in such an incident. Fitzherbert's right hand reveals a huge island (restriction and, in this case, imprisonment) beginning at around age 49, when the frenzied knife attack took place. (Astrologers may be interested to note that Fitzherbert's birth data – as given by him – are 22:15 on 26 March 1949 in Bromley, England. The attack was estimated to have taken place between 25 February and 2 March 1998, with a New Moon occurring at the position of his own Moon at the bottom of his horoscope.) Motive was never established and the prosecution had no witnesses, no exact circumstances or time of death, yet

DNA evidence linked him irrefutably to the crime. Held in custody from the time of his arrest in July, he will have to serve 15 years before being eligible for parole.

Please note that islands are not as common in prisoners' hands as one might expect. Only those who have tremendous difficulty adapting to life on the inside are likely to have an island.

c. Islands on the Heart Line

These are common at the beginning of the Heart Line under the little and ring fingers. They can reflect growing pains, difficult emotional teenage transitions and the loss of a first love.

d. Island on the Head Line

Although this is a sign of great intelligence, it indicates that we suffer from stress when meeting deadlines or being put under any sort of pressure. When the island lies under the line, we feel isolated and stressed primarily by our personal or relationship problems. When the island sits on top of the line it, reveals stress and problems lying predominantly in our professional sphere. Very often the island is central and shows that our stresses affect all areas of our life. See examples on pages 133 and 168, and for further information see page 168.

Palm Print 29
A large island on the Life Line, between the approximate ages of 30 and 40.

e. Island on the Fate Line or Apollo Line

It is rare to see an island on either of these lines, but it would concur with a loss of reputation or with creative frustration. This marking can tell of a period of uncertainty about our life path, of feeling dissatisfied in the workplace, or of feeling burdened by the workload.

I remember seeing an island in the Fate Line of a client who was in her late twenties and enjoying a fair amount of success in her media-related field. The island was to occur between the ages of 32 and 34. This suggested a period when she would feel restricted, bored or generally unhappy at work. With this foresight, instead of being blind to her predicament, she was able to make a tricky transition into another field without enduring two years of unnecessary frustration. This illustrates how we need not feel victims of future events shown in the hands, but can take advantage of the knowledge to avoid potential problems.

Timing on the Life Line

The Life Line is usually timed downwards, although some palmists look at the end of the line at the base upwards to discover clues about the childhood. View the Life Line as a journey down into the palm. Look, for example, to see if its flow is impeded and whether it moves further into the palm or retreats towards the thumb.

There are numerous ways to time this line, but I've always divided the line into segments of seven years, with 21 being almost directly below the edge of the index finger, and 35 being on a direct line from under the little finger towards the Life Line. Often this intersects the Head and Fate Lines, but not when these are higher on the hand or missing in part. Please remember that the length of the Life Line does not represent our longevity, but represents the quality of our life. Note that the Mars line can be timed using the Life Line gauge.

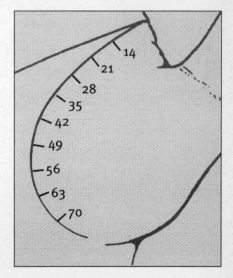

Lines that cross the Life Line

Time these lines as described above and, as with any minor lines and markings, check to see whether the Life Line continues unchanged, or has been irrevocably changed after this interruption, either by becoming stronger or weaker.

- **A line on the Mount of Venus cutting the Life Line and heading towards (or connecting to) the Heart Line:** this is a sign of a personal relationship that influences us greatly. See Relationship Lines, pages 134–8.

- **A line rising from within the early part of the Life Line, cutting the Life Line and heading in the direction of the middle finger:** this can represent a difficult experience in youth that involved a shock, a

Palm Print 30
Lines crossing the Life Line

The owner of this print has two lines cutting the Life Line at 28 and 31. At 28 he fractured his neck and three years later underwent emergency surgery when doctors discovered a genetic disorder after a hernia operation. This print was taken six months later. Note the String of Pearls effect (see page 163) in the centre of the hand, pointing to continuing weak health. He was told that he would never fully recover.

sudden accident or the death of a loved one.

During one of my first-ever professional readings I found this mark and told the client there had been a family shock that affected him deeply at the age of 21 for a number of years (an island followed the crossing line on the Life Line). With a statement like that you are either right or wrong – I was too green to realise the limb I'd gone out on! At the end of the reading he remarked that when he was 21 his brother had drowned.

- **Lines reaching the Life Line or cutting the Mars Line (see page 170) originating from the direction of the thumb:** these are family and personal events that affect us deeply. The larger ones can show up as Heartbreak Lines (see page 150).

- **A clear line cutting the Life Line usually from the direction of the middle finger:** this is an accident or illness prone time, so we must take care of our bodies and not become involved in risky pursuits or dangerous sports.

Timing on the Head Line

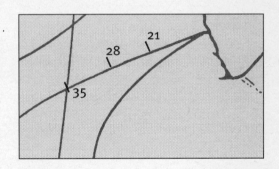

Most palmists read the Head Line from under the index finger out into the palm. Markings and changes on the Head Line reveal disruptions or major shifts in perspective, approach or opinion. The course of the Head Line also describes the process that our thinking takes. Do we curb a natural instinct to jump to conclusions? Do we make quick decisions then look for confirmation?

When the Head Line is attached to the Life Line, we start out carefully assessing a situation; we're prudent, cautious and circumspect (see page 57 for more details). The age at which the lines separate indicates the beginning of greater confidence and independence, often both physically and psychologically.

Palm Profile 2 shows many of the features that can be seen on the Head Line.

Catherine

This print belongs to Catherine, a highly intelligent woman who, through hard work and determination, survived highly competitive environments to teach French literature and the French language at some of England's most prestigious universities. The course of Catherine's long, straight Head Line not only reveals her method of analysing situations and formu-lating ideas, it also reveals key periods of change in her life. Let's examine this fascinating line.

Catherine described her thinking/working process to me:

- She sits down, clears space around her, makes sure she is not disturbed, researches at length with numerous books, loses herself in her work (a, b, c), then there's an intuitive leap where the idea clicks to offer her a way forward (d).

- At school Catherine was gifted, clever and academic (a, b). One year ahead in her studies and the youngest in the class, she was always quick to grasp the complexities of a subject (particularly languages) and absorb information (a). She passed her exams with distinction at 18 (b).

- Yet external events (c, d) conspired to hold her back from accomplishing more, and she found herself at a new school, having to prove herself once again. Catherine described her academic life as 'jumping hurdles early on' (b), then encountering unexpected delays and setbacks (c) and then having to re-jump more hurdles to prove herself and catch up (d).

Other markings to note:

- The series of fine dots in between the overlapping Head Lines: she suffers from migraine.

- Two branches rise from the Head Line towards the ring and little fingers in her mid-30s: she gave up teaching to concentrate on raising her children at 34 (branch to ring finger) and was, for a while, able to be supported by her husband, due to his improved financial position (branch to little finger).

- The long space between the base of the index finger and the thumb confirms her love of reading.

- The new Head Line beginning at approximately 38: this was the year she began studying astrology.

- The break in the Fate Line below the Heart Line, with the new line taking over: at age 48, after studying the subject for a number of years, she took exams in astrology. Teaching the subject would later become her main career avenue.

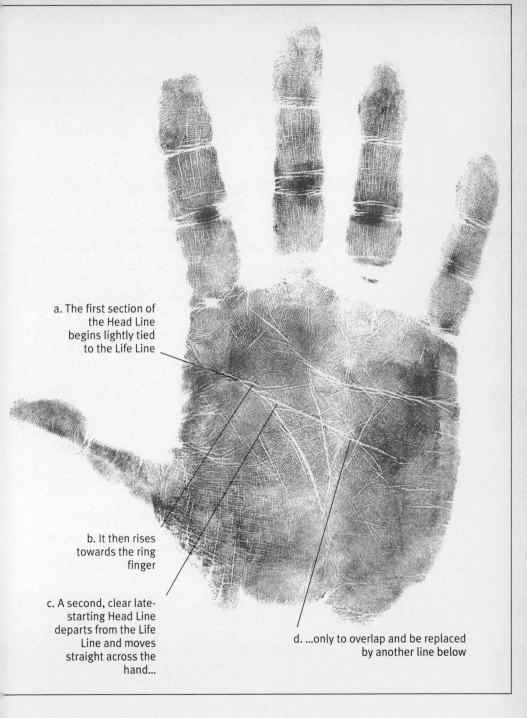

a. The first section of the Head Line begins lightly tied to the Life Line

b. It then rises towards the ring finger

c. A second, clear late-starting Head Line departs from the Life Line and moves straight across the hand...

d. ...only to overlap and be replaced by another line below

Timing on the Fate and Apollo Lines

Most palmists read the Fate Line from near the wrist upwards. If we can master timing this most interesting line we can also time other lines that join or run parallel to it. The Apollo Line (running up to the ring finger), Travel Lines (on the edge of the palm) and Influence Lines joining the Fate Line can all be timed using the timing scale of the Fate Line. When assessing the Fate Line, be careful not to confuse a diagonal-looking Fate Line with a Head Line that splits in two or sends a strong branch downwards.

Interestingly, the Fate Line will often not begin when we join the workforce, but when we develop a routine, structure and plan for our long-term goals, security and responsibilities. It is more likely to appear (or to strengthen) when

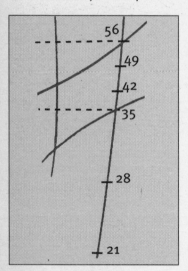

we leave home or college or take on a mortgage. The line begins at the time we feel we are developing lasting foundations, stronger commitments and security. It can coincide with the moment we feel we have arrived, we have understood a long-term plan, or we are working to pay the bills for the first time. Often the careers of child performers – and others who work from an early age – will be shown by branches rising early from the Life Line or Head Line. When they move into a more regular path and routine, the Fate Line often begins.

Where does the Fate Line originate?

The higher up in the hand the Fate Line starts, the later we formulate our goals and ambitions into a constructive plan. This is often due to early family restrictions or interference. The lower the line, the earlier we settle ourselves into a fixed pattern, routine or set of responsibilities.

High Head Lines or Head Lines that are separated from the Life Line can offset timing the Fate Line. As with the Simian Line (see page 134), try to find a centre point (this will usually be half a centimetre under the Head Line) and call it 35.

From the outer side of the palm

When the Fate Line begins from the lower, outer side of the palm, we often work directly with the public or rely on them for our income (from acting to waiting tables – or perhaps both if we choose the acting profession). Many of us love working with people and can use a strong feeling for the public pulse to our advantage (particularly if we have whorls on our fingers, indicating foresight). When the Fate Line or Apollo Line sweeps in from a higher position on the outer side of the palm, there is public recognition or a feeling of being appreciated later in our career.

From the Life Line

When the Fate Line rises from inside the Life Line (on the Mount of Venus) or when it is tied closely to the lower end of the Life Line (see Palm Print 4(a)), we feel naturally responsible and committed to helping our family. We can be too dependent and need time to separate ourselves from early family commitments and pressures and may start our true life path a little later than most. We sometimes follow in the family business or our work is closely tied to the family. Occasionally there will be financial backing, but more often than not duty to family has dominated our early life.

 A client of mine, a film director in his mid-30s, asked when he would achieve his breakthrough. He had a number of scripts but no backing from investors. His hands showed a new Fate Line appearing at the age of 38, sweeping from the outer side of the palm (high up on the Mount of Luna). I suggested that this would be the time when his career was given a boost by extra funding. At 37 he began receiving a new level of financial backing for his projects, which led to his first feature film the following year.

When the Fate Line rises from higher up the Life Line, we are determined, self-made self-starters who are not afraid to begin again away from family influence and forge our own path. This is a mark of the late developer who eventually finds independence. When the line begins higher up on the Life Line, we may worry that we have missed the boat but should understand that our life experience up to this age will play an invaluable role in future dealings.

A new start, when the Fate Line rises from the Life Line, should be timed using the Fate Line timing map, not that of the Life Line.

When does the career end or change?

It is not easy to assess the likely end of someone's working life until we understand their character and temperament. Nevertheless, the Fate Line will show important life path changes. At the age where the line ends we feel that our routine has ended, life is not such a 9 to 5 struggle and we can relax more. In Diagram 7 we can see that using this timing system the Fate Line meets the Head Line at approximately 35. A Fate Line that ends here, is traditionally considered a sign of a mistake that ends the career, but I believe it to indicate the start of a new life (possibly beginning a family) where the demands and

The Fate Line usually changes shape at around the age of 29 (coinciding with the astrologically significant Saturn Return) and around the mid-30s. Both periods are synonymous with work-family decisions and restlessness. At these times we feel the need to take stock of our lives – Gail Sheehy in *New Passages* describes this as a time for 'taking inventory'. Now that people are finding new employment in their 50s and 60s we can expect this new surge of effort to be reflected in the development of the Fate Line above the Heart Line, and in more energy being shown in the later stages of the Life Line. The age of 35 is an important crossroads and is usually shown by the intersection of the Head and Fate Lines. When the Fate Line moves past this point we have usually made up our mind (Head Line) about our responsibilities and life path (Fate Line).

priorities change. Traditionally, the end of the Fate Line at the Heart Line was the sign of a mistake in love that ends the career. Again, using the timing shown in Diagram 7, this would occur around the age of 56, and I find that it more often indicates an early retirement.

Lines crossing the Fate Line

These often indicate interference from others that causes stress. Often the obstacles need careful handling. Look to see where the crossing lines originate from: from the direction of the thumb they indicate family influences, from the outer edge of the hand they show work stresses. Look at the section on Relationship Lines (pages 134–8) to find out more.

When the Fate Line takes over from a short Life Line

Don't be worried that a short Life Line signifies a short life. It doesn't. Look to the Fate Line, as it will often act as a new Life Line, particularly when it wraps around the base of the thumb.

This formation can show that our routine and life as they have been up until this point may come to an end. We must be able to move on, relying upon inner reserves of strength to get through this difficult period of adjustment. In the two examples in Palm Print 31, Palm A is a businessman who gave up working for other people to branch out on his own at the age of 50. Palm B is a woman whose routine and life evaporated at around the same time that her husband died. She went through a difficult period of depression and, in her own words, it took everything she had to get out of bed every morning and face another day.

Palm Print 31
Examples of the Fate Line taking over from the Life Line

Palm A

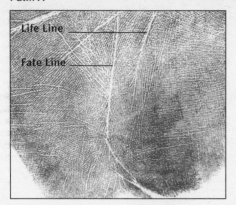

Palm B

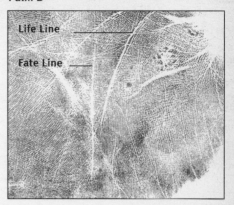

Putting It Together

Palm Profiles 3 and 4 show how we can put together all the information we have learned so far to pinpoint life events on the major lines.

Often a print will reveal strengths and weaknesses on a particular line that are difficult to see by looking directly at the hand. For example, a period on a palm print when the Fate Line is faint may reveal times when we concentrate less on goals, when we lack motivation, or when our work life is not as busy as it once was.

Alternatively, times when the Fate Line appears particularly strong can show periods when all we do is work, when we pour our energies into achieving something in the eyes of the world. During this period we may keep working for little personal reward or satisfaction.

If our ambitions and work are all-consuming (as revealed by a strong Head Line in a print), a strong Fate Line print shows that we are determined to succeed, our schedule becomes the driving force of our life, and other matters (including friendships) may be neglected. At best we realise how close we are to accomplishing our life goals.

When our aim is to achieve worldly success or creative fulfilment, however, a weak period on the Fate Line will show that relationships distract us. Perhaps we are not in demand as much in our careers at the time, there is little to motivate us, or the work dissatisfies us and boredom sets in.

A Life in Lines

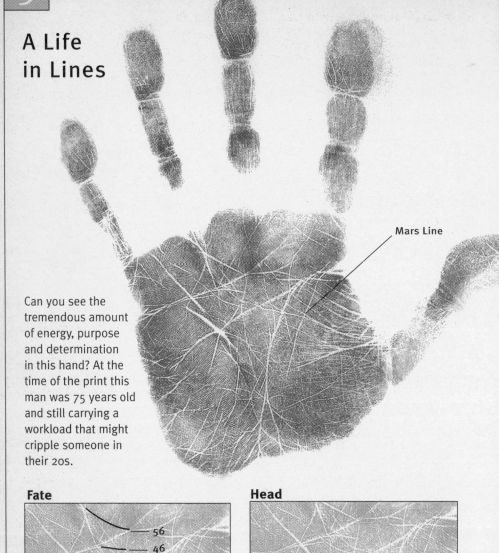

Mars Line

Can you see the tremendous amount of energy, purpose and determination in this hand? At the time of the print this man was 75 years old and still carrying a workload that might cripple someone in their 20s.

Fate

— 56
— 46

— 28

Head

47 38

Main features of the hand

- The thumb is very large, and the lines are clear and strong. This man is capable of putting his mind to almost anything and succeeding.

- The Head Line is long and straight, breaks away from the Life Line later than usual and ends in a large fork, indicating a cautious, tactical and intelligent mind but one that can be self-destructive (the large fork).

- The straight Head Line reveals a rational, practical, mentality with a prove-it-to-me attitude.

- As the Life and Head Lines separate, a long branch extends to both the index and middle fingers – a sign of great ambition and responsibility (note, too, the number of rising lines from the Life Line to the middle finger). This man always wants to improve himself and makes considerable efforts to do so.

- The presence of a strong Mars Line (see page 170) with the square palm points to an aggressive, bellicose temperament.

- The numerous lines from the Mount of Lower Mars inside the Life Line point to personal events (see below).

Life

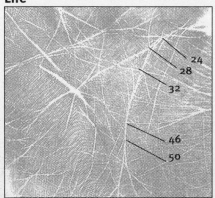

Timing

Let's look at the various markings on each line to see how they create a fuller picture of this man's life:

LIFE

17 – Rising line: leaves home and cycles in competitions

24 – A line heading from Mars towards the Heart Line: marries

28 – Rising line to index and middle finger: night-school classes in law and mechanical engineering

32 – Rising line to middle finger: begins new job

46 – Cutting line: fired from job

50 – Descending lines towards the Mount of Luna: new life with third wife

FATE

28 – Rising from Life Line: night-school classes

46 – Crossing line: fired from job

56 – Strong branch to ring finger: reputation and finances improve

HEAD

38 – Branch towards little finger: meets second wife

47 – Branch from middle finger: begins his own company

MARS

35 – Cutting line: father dies

41 – Cutting line: separates from first wife

49 – Cutting line: widowed

Bouncing Back

This print was taken a number of years ago, after Antonia had suffered a breakdown from stress.

Main features of the hand

- The hand shape fits the element of Water, revealing Antonia's emotional sensitivity and receptivity. Water hands may suffer from stress-related illnesses and breakdowns more than the other hand types because they can be impressionable and vulnerable. Yet water is the strongest element because of its non-resistance; as an element, water is passive to external events – it simply absorbs.

- There is an over-heavy Mars Line (see page 170) but a feathery Life Line. At the time of this print Antonia was coping with a build-up of anger, resentment and aggression which, combined with a number of stressful situations, resulted in a breakdown described by doctors as 'psychotic'. In a recent print the Life and Mars Lines had become more equal in strength.

- The long index finger shows pride, ambition and confidence, but the island in the Head Line points to uncertainty and self-doubt, thus undermining the qualities of a long index finger.

- There is an intelligent but sensitive Head Line.

Timing

- The overlap in the Head Line occurs between the ages of 27 and 31, when Antonia divorced, redefined her goals and became a stronger, more resilient person.

- The Fate Line makes fascinating reading. It overlaps between the ages of 31 and 33, with the second line heading towards the index finger. Between these years Antonia slowly assumed a leadership (index) role in her business, when the senior partner moved into retirement.

- The first, more marked, Fate Line also has numerous branch lines joining and rising from it. The first (a) at 28 coincided with a greater sense of freedom after Antonia's divorce. At 29 (b) and 30 (c) new relationships began, the latter inspiring a rising branch line in

the direction of the ring finger, pointing to greater personal fulfilment. Finally (d) a rising line (and the new Fate Line) signalled greater happiness, self-determination and control of her own life. At 31 Antonia began to take over the responsibility of running the company and moved house.

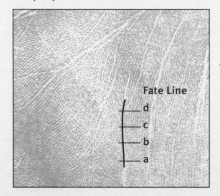

Fate Line
d
c
b
a

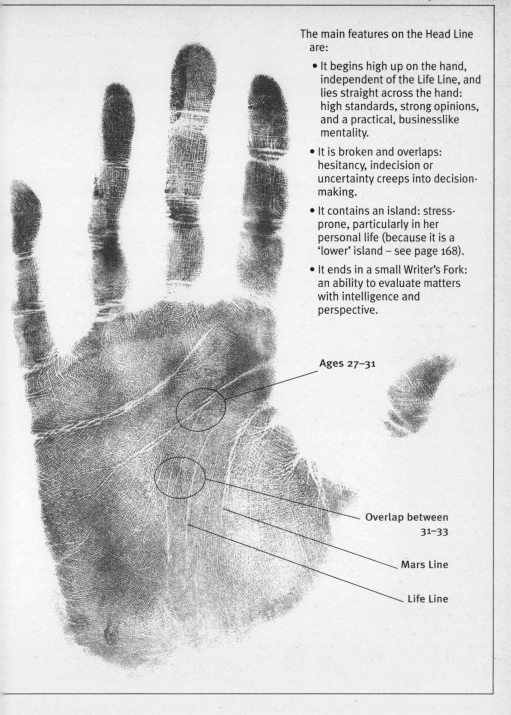

The main features on the Head Line are:

- It begins high up on the hand, independent of the Life Line, and lies straight across the hand: high standards, strong opinions, and a practical, businesslike mentality.

- It is broken and overlaps: hesitancy, indecision or uncertainty creeps into decision-making.

- It contains an island: stress-prone, particularly in her personal life (because it is a 'lower' island – see page 168).

- It ends in a small Writer's Fork: an ability to evaluate matters with intelligence and perspective.

Ages 27–31

Overlap between 31–33

Mars Line

Life Line

Timing Other Lines

The Heart Line

I wouldn't advise timing this line – I've found it far too unreliable, but try it for yourself. Some palmists use a 10-year gauge, starting at the age of 15 (directly under the little finger), then moving to 25 (under the gap between the little and middle fingers) and so on.

The Simian Line

This will often disrupt the timing of the Fate Line. There may be no easy way to time the Fate Line when you come across someone with a Simian Line, but I suggest that you take a central point in the palm and assign it the age of 35. You'll learn more if you ask the person about career and life events and you'll be able to gauge this better. Saying that, people with Simian Lines tend to march to a different drummer so it can be difficult to predict for them. Their lives appear to be a build-up of events and reactions. But remain flexible and listen to their stories.

Relationship Lines

Relationships can be found in various sections of the hand. The most well-known, yet least reliable, of these lines are the Gypsy Relationship Lines (see pages 135–6), which lie under the little finger. But before learning how to time these lines there are some points to remember.

- These lines are not reliable indicators as to the extent or number of our partners.

- The same partner can show twice (when the relationship begins a new phase; for example, when a business partner becomes a lover).

- The lines don't always represent actual relationships. They can be in our mind: the attractive shop assistant we fantasise about but only meet every morning when buying a coffee, the celebrity we're obsessed with but never get close to.

- Relationship Lines on the left hand demonstrate more clearly our deeper love commitments.

- The lines don't show marriage, but rather relationship commitments.

- *The strength and length of the lines are relative to the depth of our feelings, regardless of the time spent in the actual relationship.*

Timing Relationship Lines is difficult. Some palmists divide them into three sections: from the Heart Line to a third of the way up represents the years up to 25; the next section shows the years until 50; the final section indicates the rest of the life. In addition, the lines can be spread out, making timing even more difficult to ascertain.

Types of Relationship Line

The different types of Relationship Line are shown in Diagrams 10 and 11. The letters in the descriptions that follow refer to features shown in Diagram 11.

Gypsy Lines

These horizontal lines are found on the outer edge of the hand, beneath the little finger and above the Heart Line and should be examined from the outer edge of the palm inwards.

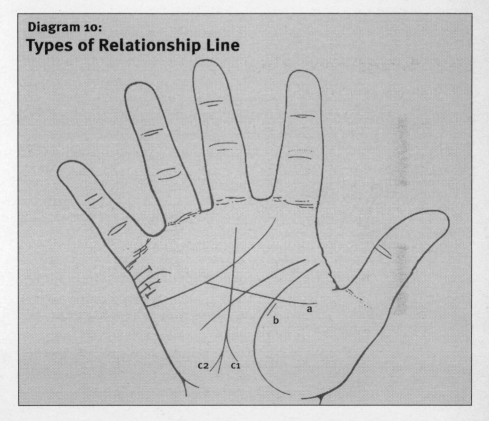

Diagram 10:
Types of Relationship Line

- Deep line (usually the top line): an emotionally significant union
- Long, straight line: strong and important
- Very thick: intense and all-consuming to the detriment of the rest of our life
- Very thin: we are not connected emotionally, or we are also in another relationship
- Only one line, beginning higher up: we get involved for other reasons than love – often an agreement to have a companion or just settling for someone
- Beginning in a fork: two separate starts to the relationship

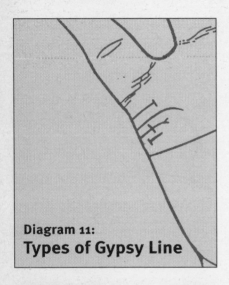

Diagram 11:
Types of Gypsy Line

Short-lived teenage crushes are shown by low-set Gypsy Lines (see page 135) just above the Heart Line. If these are still strong into our 30s we still have this person on our mind – perhaps there are unresolved matters in the relationship.

The following can be found in Diagram 11:

- Ending in a fork: often a divorce or going separate ways
- Sloping downwards or a cross ends the line: a possible loss of a loved one; possibly outliving partner
- Has a cutting line through it: disruption during the relationship
- Cutting line at the beginning (outer edge): in some way fated not to last
- Cutting line ends the line: sudden end to the partnership

Other Relationship lines

The following lines (shown in Diagram 10) are not always present on the hand, particularly if there are few lines.

a. A line from or crossing Life Line towards Heart Line

This is a most important significator of a relationship commitment, although may not be present on some hands. Sometimes it is

Palm Print 32
A Relationship Line
This shows an important
relationship that begins at
age 28 (using the Life Line
timing gauge).

broken in reaching towards the Heart Line, on other occasions it is clear. A
broken line is more likely to indicate a separation, but we should look for confirmation or otherwise by examining other factors in the hand (in particular the Fate
and Head lines). See Palm Print 32.

b. A small line running close inside Life Line

Take care not to mistake this for the Mars Line (see page 170). These lines
represent people who greatly influence the direction we take in life. They can be
lovers, mentors or important friends who share a particular time of our lives.
Some palmists call them kindred spirits with whom we share an intensity and
bond for the duration of that line. When the line ends, the situation either ends or
takes on another form. On the left hand only, this is an intensely personal asso-
ciation that doesn't affect our professional lives or is a secret. On the right hand
only, we may meet someone who teaches or inspires us but is not connected to
our personal life. This should be timed as we time the Life Line.

c. An Influence Line joining the Fate Line

When we have a relationship line that joins our Fate Line we can expect our
partners to have a great influence in shaping our life path. When the line comes
from the direction of the thumb (c1) it can show that the partner comes from
within the social or family circle, and when it comes from the outer edge of the
hand (c2) the partner comes from other areas such as work.

This type of line is particularly evident in those cultures that arrange marriages for their children. I've found that arranged unions are shown by rising lines from the thumb side. Love matches can be foretold by lines rising from the direction of outer side of the palm to the Fate Line.

From when do we time the union? When the line appears (using the Fate Line timing gauge) we are seeking a new partner, and when it touches the Fate Line the partnership becomes official (this may be an engagement, a marriage or a first meeting, dependent upon the individual's idea of what constitutes a commitment). If the line does not reach the Fate Line or travels through it, this can indicate that the partnership may be called off before it becomes official.

Children Lines
• Fine, often curved, lines just inside the Life Line
These lines appear at the age we have children, as timed using the Life Line timing gauge. The old gypsy method examines vertical lines rising off the Relationship Lines and found under the little finger, as mentioned earlier. Strong ones are supposed to represent boys, whilst light markings are girls!

Be aware that children indicated in the hand may not be your own, they could be adopted, nieces and nephews, a neighbour's child and so on. I never read children in the hand, mainly because of an early experience where a client took my comments to mean something quite different. When asked if she was going to have children, I explained that they were supposed to be located under the little finger but she had numerous fine lines and I told her I didn't know if they were children or not. After she left the reading she told a mutual friend that I had foretold miscarriages in her hand.

QUICK QUIZ 4
How would the following be best seen in a hand?

1. Unemployment or a work upheaval.

2. Academic success or a need for independence.

3. A preoccupation with financial security and making money.

4. A period of physical restriction or ill-health.

5. A stress-prone character.

(Answers in Appendix 3, page 218.)

Part 3

LOVE, HEALTH AND CAREER

Whenever people come for a palm reading, most of them will want to know about matters of love, work, money and health. When we are looking for features on the hand that relate to these issues, it is important to remember that palmistry depends on the successful interpretation of a number of different factors, which should be looked at together rather than singly.

Love and Friendship

We have already looked at Relationship Lines in 'Timing Techniques' (pages 134–8), but there are many other lines and features in the hand that show our approach to relationships, whether with friends, family or lovers.

Generosity, Warmth and Openness

Generosity will permeate all our thoughts and actions, just as those who are mean tend to be mean in everything. There are measures of carefulness with money, but true generosity or meanness is a character-defining trait. It's rarely a matter of our current finances, although childhood poverty can make those of us who are naturally generous surprisingly 'careful' with small things whilst we are giving with larger gifts.

The signs illustrated in Diagram 12 indicate generosity, warmth and openness, but these should not be considered independently – the greater the number of these markings, the more generous, warm or open we are. We can also therefore conclude that fewer of these signs indicate more of a stingy nature, as do many of the opposite signs (for example, narrow as opposed to broad nails).

Friendship Lines

As it takes time and a generous spirit to enjoy on-going relationships with friends, mean people rarely have friends for long or are not motivated to make them. Friendship Lines are interesting markings found further down on the Mount of Venus (under the thumb) running parallel to the Life Line. (Don't mistake these for the Mars Line (see page 170), which adds vigour and vitality to the personality.) These fine vertical lines show the main (usually platonic)

Diagram 12:

Signs of generosity, warmth and openness

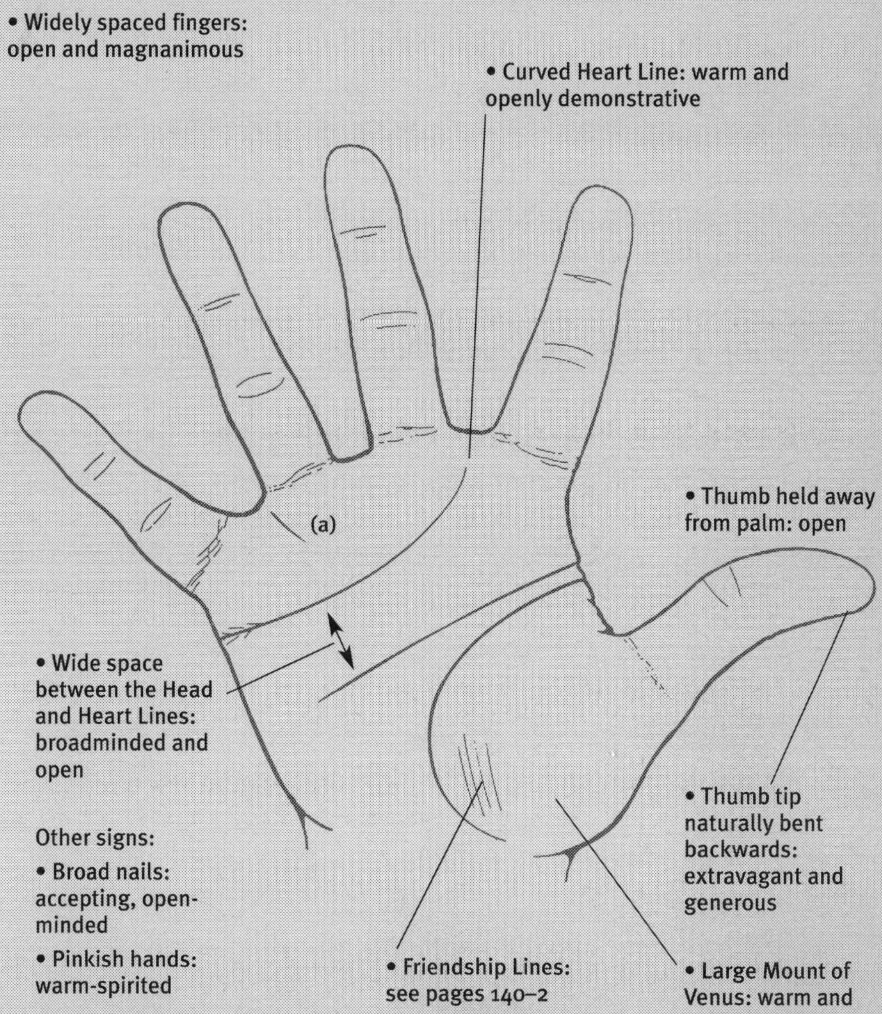

• Widely spaced fingers: open and magnanimous

• Curved Heart Line: warm and openly demonstrative

(a)

• Thumb held away from palm: open

• Wide space between the Head and Heart Lines: broadminded and open

Other signs:

• Broad nails: accepting, open-minded

• Pinkish hands: warm-spirited

• Friendship Lines: see pages 140–2

• Thumb tip naturally bent backwards: extravagant and generous

• Large Mount of Venus: warm and sensual

companions in our life – often the ones who have the deepest impact and the loyal confidants who stay with us through both good times and bad.

According to hand analyst Malcolm Wright, friends in later life can also be found on the hand as descending lines from the gap in between the little and ring fingers (shown as (a) in Diagram 12).

Signs of privacy and secretiveness

These are the major markings of privacy and secretiveness in the hand.

- A short ring finger
- Fingers held closely together
- The thumb held closely to the palm
- Closely tied Head and Life Lines
- Straight Head and/or Heart Lines
- Head and Heart Lines close together

Empathy, Self-Understanding and Sensitivity

We need a healthy degree of self-understanding before we can understand or help others, and we need to be able to listen to others, very often without giving advice. We all like to think of ourselves as sensitive people (and this may be true if we have many fine lines on the hand), but there's a world of difference between being sensitive to the remarks and opinions of others and showing sensitivity and compassion towards others. For example, loop finger prints are indicators of people who like people, but this is not a guarantee of empathy or sympathy.

Signs of empathy, self-understanding and sensitivity

Some of the signs that demonstrate a greater connection to people are shown in Diagram 13. In the list below, the letters refer to Diagram 13.

a. **A short line coming down from between the index and middle fingers:** according to hand analyst Malcolm Wright this indicates that we understand ourselves emotionally.

b. **The Medical Stigmata:** we are good listeners and healers who would do well in the caring professions on a one-to-one level. Hand analyst Ed Campbell suggests we try herbal medicines rather than homeopathic remedies if we have the marking with a bar connecting the lines.

c. **Solomon's Ring:** this confers a psychological understanding of other people (and ourselves) because we love to look beyond what people

Diagram 13:
Signs of empathy, self-understanding and sensitivity

• Short little finger: an empathy with children; a possible vocation as a parent or primary school teacher

• Branch sloping from the Heart Line to Life Line: great sensitivity to hurt, criticism and rejection; compassion

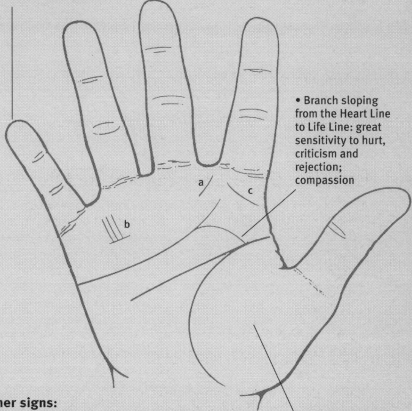

Other signs:

• Sensitivity Pads (raised mounds of flesh on the fingertips): tactile; attuned to atmospheres and others' emotions; a love for the feel of textures too

• Girdle of Venus (see page 145): heightened sensitivity, empathy and near-telepathic abilities

•Large Mount of Venus: the ability to give and receive much love and affection, but may also be needy

say, probing further to expose hidden motivations and personality characteristics. Whether we're an amateur psychologist and lend friends a sympathetic ear or we do this professionally, we have a sense of knowing what makes others tick. We impart wisdom and the benefit of our life experience to others. When this Ring is connected to the Heart Line we can provide greater emotional support to those in need, and we may be considered humanitarians, for we are genuinely fond of others. With this extra feature we can make a living out of nurturing, counselling or helping people overcome relationship or sexual problems. It is interesting to note that Cynthia Payne, the Madam of Streatham, has this feature on both hands. When the Ring connects up to a Teacher's Square (see Palm Profile 5 on pages 148–9), we can be an important influence on others and can act as a mentor.

Relationships and Sexuality

A loving relationship is the result of an exchange between two people and is a product of time. Although love may manifest itself in wonderful gifts like surprises, presents and special moments that we never forget, true love is something that grows in our hearts day by day in a secret, quiet way, often without our understanding it. More than enthusiasm and romanticism, love is the sense of belonging we have, the sense of completeness and the understanding of how much we share our completeness with our partner.

Check if the Heart Line is set high up or low down to see whether we have genuine empathy or whether we are the do-gooders, the advice givers or the incessant reassuring head-nodders. The lower the Heart Line, the more sympathetic we are – always happy to listen and provide constructive feedback. Some of us with a high Heart Line help others in order to reassure ourselves. We are less interested in others' emotional monologues and in helping them with their problems. When the Heart Line is forming a part or full Simian Line it is not considered low-set and this description may not apply.

Many psychologists believe that we love others the way we've been loved by our parents. First and foremost we must find a way of loving and expressing our needs, then if we are lucky we find someone who can be loved in the same way.

Our Head and Heart Lines (pages 52–65) reveal much about our attitude and personal needs in love and relationships. These lines should be understood fully if we wish to understand our approach to a relationship and our personal needs. For additional information, check out the palm shape, finger length (irregular finger length can indicate psychosexual problems), the Mount of Venus and the finger prints.

There are, however, a number of additional signs that reveal more complex relationship and sexual needs. These are shown in Diagram 14 and listed below. These are signs I discovered from working with many clients when I began to understand that people stay in relationships for many different reasons.

A wide space between the Head and Heart Lines

This shows a lack of repression. We prefer to be unconventional and we have pride in our broad-minded approach to relationships. (Repressed types tend to hold their fingers and thumbs close together and often have narrow palms and narrow spaces between the Head and Heart Lines, revealing a tendency to fall back into narrow-minded assumptions or to be embarrassed by public displays of affection. With the ring and middle fingers close together there can be a guilt complex about sex. Some of these people prefer to be voyeurs rather than participants.)

The Girdle of Venus

This line, which is rare in its complete form, was given a bad press in old palmistry textbooks, where someone with this line was said to be insatiable or promiscuous. Nowadays we can examine the characteristics of those with this line with greater accuracy. When the line is present but not fully formed it shows a craving for excitement and external stimuli. We need things to look forward to and may be people of extremes, overreacting emotionally to situations. Our love life may be less than simple because we need unusual people who can satisfy our needs. We are highly sexual and love sex games and variety.

When the line is fully formed there is a psychic awareness, intensity and possibly a strong musical or artistic talent. (For more details see pages 164 and 182.)

The notorious cult leader Charles Manson, who incited his followers to commit brutal murders, has a Fire hand with a strong branch line from his Head and Life Lines to the middle finger, joining a dominant Girdle of Venus. The branch line sums up his life in two ways. First, he spent most of his youth in detention centres and suffering at the hands of legal authorities (middle finger), growing immune to discipline or punishment (Head Line); secondly, the worst aspects of the Girdle of Venus are demonstrated by his thrill-seeking, power-craving and promiscuous character. He famously exercised great emotional – almost hypnotic – control over his followers (Head Line and Girdle of Venus).

Diagram 14:

Signs of complex relationship needs and sexual tendencies

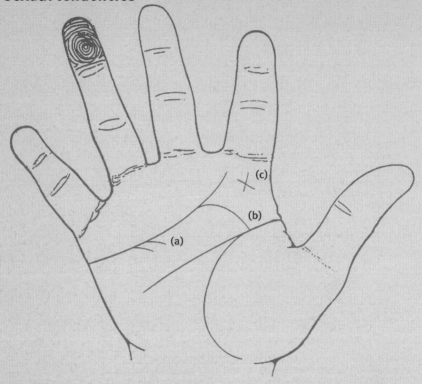

The letters in the list below refer to the signs illustrated above

a. Short sloping lines down off the Heart Line. These sometimes show disappointments in love.

b. A sloping branch from the Heart Line to the Life Line. When the Heart Line slopes or sends a strong sloping line down to the Life Line we have a fear of trusting others. Laying ourselves open to hurt makes us particularly vulnerable. We also need to be careful not to get depressed or obsessed when love ends. We may think of desperate or extreme measures to win back love or to show the other person how much we are suffering. We can use our added sensitivity to help others going through relationship problems.

c. A cross under the index finger. Traditionally a sign of a long and happy union.

Lack of commitment:

- Check the length of the middle finger: with a short finger, possibly not as faithful or committed as others

- Curved Heart Line ending under the middle finger: a lack of emotional involvement

- The little finger jutted out from the palm: unable to settle down

- A ring on the left hand little finger: a temporary problem with intimacy

Dominant or submissive:

- Check the length of the index finger: with a noticeably long or short finger, possible fantasises about dominating others or being dominated

Signs of high standards:

- A high-set Life or Head Line

- A curved Heart Line ending directly under the index finger

- Long fingers

- A Simian Line

Sensuality:

- The bottom phalange of the little finger is padded: sexy and sensual; comfortable with intimacy and with own body

- Horizontal lines across the lower section of the Mount of Venus: pleasure-seeking

- Long fingers: a desire to perfect the art of foreplay and lovemaking

Toy boy or sugar daddy:

- The index is longer than the ring finger: may need older or emotionally mature partners

- The ring finger is longer than the index finger: may seek younger partners to keep feeling youthful and active

Signs of spontaneity and an 'anything goes' attitude:

- Widely spaced fingers

- A curved Heart Line

- The thumb is held away from the palm

- A wide space between the Head and Heart Lines (see page 141)

- Long fingers: a willingness to explore sexual fantasies, role play and down'n' dirty activities

- A Simian Line: a possible interest in S&M activities

- A whorl on the little finger: sexually adventurous

- The Girdle of Venus (see page 145)

Signs of immaturity or ingenuousness:

- A short little finger (see diagram)

- A low-set little finger (see diagram)

- The little finger held curled into the palm

- The Fate Line tied to the lower part of the Life Line

Cross-dressing tendencies:

- A whorl on the ring finger and/or a long or pointed index finger, with a square palm and long, delicate fingers

Rosalind

This is a palm print of a successful American lawyer who is a much-respected head of her department. The hand has some interesting contradictions: the long, delicate lines (finesse, analytical ability) sitting beside the short, thick thumb (bluntness). It is an excellent example of a complex, sensitive woman who has developed confidence and a reputation on her own terms.

We can note the following:

• The Heart and Head Lines are long and gently curved. She can tackle intricate matters, and guide her staff with consideration yet continue to be a lateral-thinking (curved Head Line) executive who wins major client accounts. These lines reveal an excellent tactician able to anticipate the long-term view and act accordingly. She can compromise or put pressure on her opponents without making them feel cornered. She describes herself as non-confrontational but wilful. (Note the whorl on the index finger, which also tells of personal integrity.)

• The Heart Line ends by sending a branch down to the Life Line and forming a Teacher's Square. This shows high personal sensitivity and an ability to understand the anxieties of others. At work she is best known for her intensive teaching and mentoring, having realised the importance of training her staff to be compassionate and insightful when working with clients. This is a method she developed from stressful times working for employers whose methods of leadership were antagonistic and ultimately counterproductive. For more on the Teacher's Square see page 186.

• The Head Line contains an island and descending branch lines. These reveal a number of the professional stresses this woman has endured, as well as an early lack of self-confidence. Its feathery descending lines in the early 30s and an island in early adulthood (18 to 21) coincide with difficult periods of adjustment. The line strengthens by the mid-30s and, with a long index finger and strong Mars Line, she has blossomed into an effective and motivational boss.

• There is an eye formation at the end of the Head Line. From childhood she has had numerous difficulties with her sight and has had corrective eye surgery on both eyes (the left hand also contains this large island).

Looking to the future we can see an end to the main Fate Line and the start of two paths in the late 30s/early 40s. This adjustment may be difficult because the Life Line ends in a square and is taken over by the main Fate Line. Note that the inner 'Life' line is, in fact, a strong Mars Line.

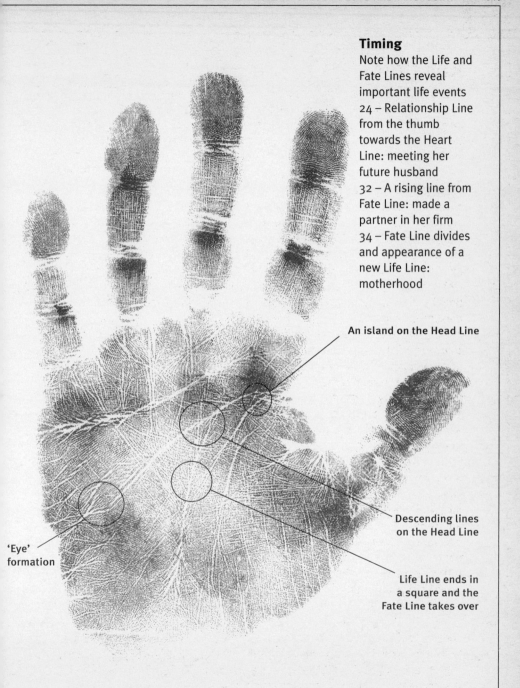

Timing
Note how the Life and Fate Lines reveal important life events
24 – Relationship Line from the thumb towards the Heart Line: meeting her future husband
32 – A rising line from Fate Line: made a partner in her firm
34 – Fate Line divides and appearance of a new Life Line: motherhood

An island on the Head Line

Descending lines on the Head Line

'Eye' formation

Life Line ends in a square and the Fate Line takes over

The Heartbreak Line

Found on the Mount of Venus (see Palm Print 33 below), this indicates that we are currently carrying great sorrow around with us from a past loss, perhaps from a relationship ending, a partner dying or the loss of a beloved parent. Even if we lost a parent or partner many years ago, the presence of this line reveals that it still affects us.

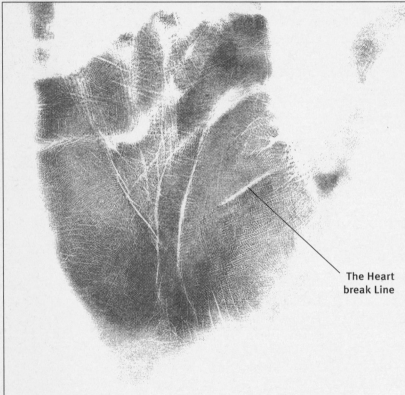

The Heart break Line

Palm Print 33
The Heartbreak Line – sorrow from a broken engagement

This is the hand of an unhappy American woman who broke off her engagement in her mid-30s to take care of her father (the middle and ring fingers are held close together). Note the ghost-like appearance of the hand, the disruption on the Fate and Head Lines at around the mid-30s. This raises an interesting question: does the Head Line swoop down into the hand (now living in a fantasy world) or is the rising Fate Line merging into the Head Line (an abrupt life change due to a decision)?

The Humanitarian Heart Line

This line is found on those of us who put other matters before our relationships; often we are considered humanitarians because of our understanding of suffering and inequality, but some of us prefer to love the human race rather than individuals. Some of us enjoy socialising but put our work needs before love, earning us the tag 'workaholic'. Hand analyst Ed Campbell describes this person as very possessive and blind to the real nature of their partner.

 The Humanitarian Heart Line is found on the hand of Bob Geldof, sometimes referred to as 'Saint Bob' for his enormous fundraising efforts for millions of starving children in Africa. Geldof's sense of moral outrage at the behaviour of politicians in the face of modern genocide is a positive example of this line.

The Humanitarian Heart Line is long and straight, and extends across the palm

Palm Print 34
The Humanitarian Heart Line

Sexual preference

No single feature on the hand can show sexual preference because sexuality is a key component of our whole personality. We can sometimes, however, get some indication from the Heart Line. As the Heart Line is formed in the womb and develop in childhood, particularly during puberty, it is logical to conclude that our sexual needs are in part genetically determined and in part the result of early interaction, socialisation and parental influence.

There is a sign that shows we are likely to have experienced *problems with or confusion over sexual orientation in childhood*. This is where the Heart Line sends a short, hook-like branch down towards the Life Line. Please note that this hook does not touch the Life Line. Perhaps same-sex preference may remain latent in us if the hook is shown only in the left hand. In this case we may fear the reactions of others or remain in the closet. We can speculate that when found only on the right hand there has been a gradual development towards homo-sexuality rather than it being the result of a genetic factor.

Signs of sexual problems

It is often said that when partners are having good sex with each other they can overcome most other problems in their relationship. Sex is said to be 90 per cent of a bad relationship and 10 per cent of a good one. The following are some signs of sexual problems.

When a palm print is taken carefully and yet the bottom phalanges of the fingers (those nearest the palm) do not show up, this may indicate that we find it difficult to let other people into our daily lives. We prefer to live in a world of our own. At worst we can shut out people on a physical and emotional level. Perhaps some previous hurt has caused us to be very wary of others or of letting ourselves get too emotionally attached. On a physical level we also need to rethink and change our current diet.

- **The little finger is curled in** (see page 86): we may have a naïve or prudish attitude to sex.

- **The left print of the little finger bottom phalange is thinner than that of the right:** if the print of the bottom phalange is thin or missing, then we are usually abstaining from sex because we need to resolve emotional or sexual repression. If you find this on your palm, have a look at the shape of your palm, the type of Heart Line you possess and the dominant finger in your hand to help uncover what you really need, sexually and emotionally, from another person.

- The left hand print of the bottom phalange of the little finger is strong and full, but the right is thin or weak: we may prefer (at this stage) not to be sexually involved with another, but rather to engage in masturbation and private fantasies. This sign can indicate a late developer or simply someone who is not having sex at present.

- **Arrows at the beginning of the Heart Line:** these indicate jealousy. This emotion can be far more destructive than envy, which at best can spur us on to improve ourselves. At worst, with this marking we can be overly possessive, unforgiving and unwilling (rather than unable) to see another's point of view.

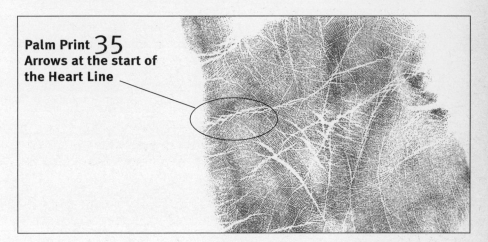

**Palm Print 35
Arrows at the start of the Heart Line**

**Palm Print 36
Relationship problems**

A print taken three months before this man decided to separate from his wife. Can you see the signs of relationship trouble and indecision in his Head Line? See the section on fuzzy Head Lines on page 180.

Becoming Accountable: Moving Away From Parental Control

Most of us reach a certain age (which often coincides with the first Saturn Return, an astrologically significant turning point in life occurring around the age of 28 to 30) when we stop blaming our parents for the mistakes they made whilst raising us, and start to accept responsibility for our own decisions and actions. Some of the following signs of parental influences in our life have already been presented in the section on 'Finger Positioning' (see pages 83–8). They show that we *can* change our existing attitudes, heal childhood scars and improve our existing relationships with parents, partners and children.

- When the ring and middle fingers are held close together (particularly if the middle finger has developed a curve) this can indicate guilt about having our own life or about feeling sexual enjoyment, or a fear of taking the plunge and leaving parental connections behind.

- When the little finger is low set (see pages 87–8) we can make unfair or destructive comparisons between our partner and a parent.

- When the Life Line begins with an island we may have felt unhappy in childhood or be searching for a missing element in the family. Some of us may have been affected by our own feelings and others' reactions to being illegitimate, but this sign's connection to illegitimacy is not as prevalent as it once was, as we now have more relaxed attitudes to childbirth out of wedlock.

- Lines rising from the Life Line to index finger, with a chain or island early in the Life Line indicate that we may have experienced a harsh or restricting childhood in which we felt misunderstood. These rising lines show our attempts to break away and seek independence.

One of the most fascinating aspects of palmistry, which we can see only from a print, is a noticeable missing section where the Life or Head Line begins (see Palm Print 36). This indicates that the person is temporarily switched off emotionally. This will show up particularly in their sex life (check the little finger and the bottom phalange near the palm to see how sexually active or aware they are). When this section is missing and the bottom phalange of the little finger is full on the print, the person has an active sex life but at present is not emotionally intimate. They may be faking it or may be unwilling to let others affect them emotionally.

- The Family Ring and Thumb Chain (two markings on the lower joint of the thumb) reveal a strong bond with the family.

- The Matriarch Line, as introduced by Ed Campbell, reveals a dominant woman in our life who may prove hard for a partner to live up to. This doubles up as an Allergy Line (see pages 164–5).

- The Heartbreak Line (see page 150) can show that we are living in the past, unable to move on after the loss of a parent.

- When the Head and Life Lines are linked together for an extended period (see page 57) we find it difficult to become emotionally independent adults.

 Both Michael Jackson and his sister Janet have complex Fate Lines, but both have main sections of the line tied to the Life Line, indicating the importance of the family structure in determining their chosen paths – as well as their need to detach themselves from it. When the Fate Line struggles up through and beyond the Life Line towards the middle finger, we can suppose there has been a great amount of effort to assert independence. These people take enormous, vital steps to break away from the family mould.

- When the Fate Line begins near the Life Line, rising from it or beginning inside it, we carry family responsibilities or expectations into adulthood.

Complex People and Reactions

We all need patience to understand difficult people, particularly those who cannot help being their own worst enemy. Here are some signs to look out for of complex or difficult people.

- The Simian Line (see pages 66–7 for complete details).

- The Head, Heart and Life Lines begin from the same point. We have a one-track mind or can be a self-saboteur. Palmist Elizabeth Daniels Squire, in *Palmistry Made Practical*, described this as a person who 'sits on a powder keg to smoke'. Author Henry Miller is one person with this sign of triple intensity.

- A double Head Line (see page 197 for details).

- Many whorl finger prints. We are often too intense and individualistic to get on with others. We can be bigots who dislike whole sections of the population because of gender, sexuality or race. We can be too demanding as well as eccentric, perverse and downright obstreperous!

- A Clubbed Thumb (see below). We are highly emotional and prone to sudden bursts of temper.

The Clubbed Thumb – the beast within

This is an unforgettable thumb tip – short, stubby and often swollen-looking. The nail is a giveaway – it is short and wide. This formation is often hereditary, from a parent or aunt/uncle of the same sex as us. With this mark we are:

- Highly emotional
- Deeply intense, tense and extreme
- Capable of erupting into sudden bursts of temper
- Stress-prone
- A perfectionist
- Controlled – to maintain self-restraint
- Easily frustrated and touchy
- An emotional pressure-cooker
- Unable to indulge in small-talk

This used to be known as the 'Murderer's Thumb' and in some ways it is a stronger manifestation of Simian Line characteristics. We may seem to have a dramatic temperament and be attention-seeking, but our problem can be more deep-rooted than this. We may spend much time controlling our emotional responses, fearing that we may explode and alienate others around us. At worst we can be violent, but usually our outbursts are in the form of tantrums. We should find constructive and creative ways of releasing our tension. We demand the very best but are frustrated by our own lack of perfection. We need space from others and appreciation for our efforts. Our conversation is always deep, meaningful, intensely personal and about matters that seem to us to be life-or-death issues.

Andrew Fitzherbert, in *Hand Psychology*, is one of the few palmists to address at length this rare feature. He attributes it to a possible brain defect and links it to a section of the brain called 'the Thumb Centre'. He suggests that those with clubbed thumbs need to avoid building up tension and find ways to relax. Fitzherbert advises friends and family not to tease, annoy or frustrate those with a clubbed thumb. Misunderstandings should be avoided or resolved quickly.

One client with two clubbed thumbs was a perfectionist who suffered from stress during the build-up to examinations. Periodically she would have tantrums, anxiety attacks, and fits of hysterical crying, and would lock herself away. She set a tremendous amount of store by succeeding and was terrified of not doing herself justice or not being seen to be fulfilling her full potential. This is an extreme example and is no doubt exaggerated by the fact that her hands belong to the element of Water.

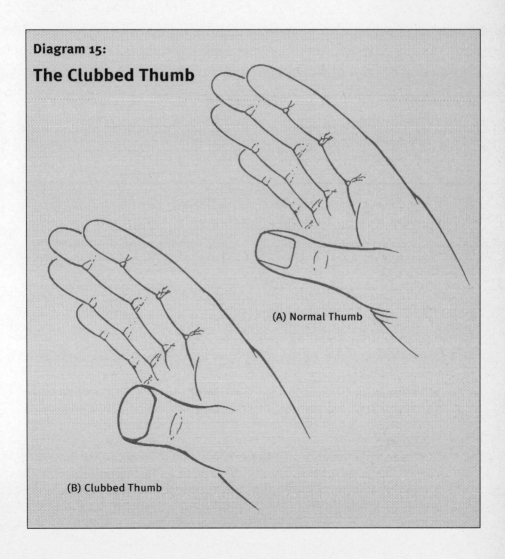

Diagram 15:

The Clubbed Thumb

(A) Normal Thumb

(B) Clubbed Thumb

Health Matters

Palmistry is increasingly being used in a medical context. Signs of health concerns can be seen on both the hands, but the left hand is more likely to show inherited health concerns. As well as studying the lines on the hand, check out the hand element type, the fingernail shape and finger prints for other health signs. See the section on 'A Measure of Energy', pages 169–71, for further analysis. And don't forget to check what happens following a particular marking – does the line improve and health is restored, or do we continue to struggle on?

We should pay particular attention to times when our prints are faint (low energy levels), lines fade (mental or physical illness – lines will reappear once our health improves) and skin ridge patterns break up (attacks on the immune system).

A Daily Health Check

For a daily health check look at the Health Line. This is the diagonal line (or series of fine lines) beginning near the little finger and heading towards the Life Line. It should be a pinkish colour. When dark or black it is indicative of great nervous strain and poor health. When it is strong on the hand (or there are a multitude of lines descending) we have a moody temperament that see-saws regularly. Numerous lines can show digestive problems, anxiety or acidity – see (b) on Diagram 16.

Look at the 'mouse', too. This is the fleshy part of the back of the hand (next to the thumb and under the index finger) formed when the thumb is pressed against the hand. The firmer the mouse, the stronger our recuperative powers and general health.

Common Signs of Health Problems

Please use the following as a guide only. This information is not intended to be taken as a replacement for professional medical advice. Any person with a condition requiring medical attention should consult a qualified practitioner or therapist.

Diagram 16 shows some of the most common signs that relate to medical conditions and states of health.

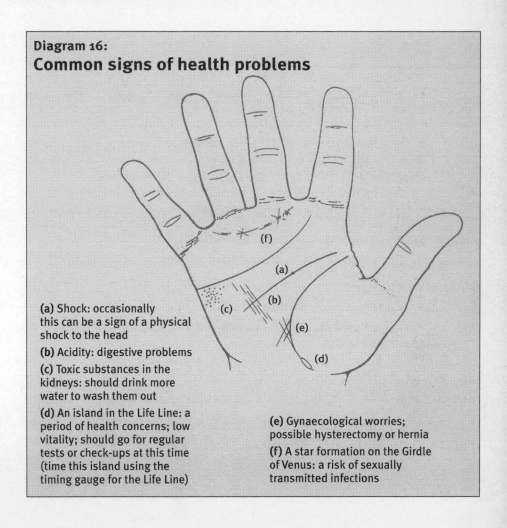

Diagram 16:
Common signs of health problems

(a) Shock: occasionally this can be a sign of a physical shock to the head

(b) Acidity: digestive problems

(c) Toxic substances in the kidneys: should drink more water to wash them out

(d) An island in the Life Line: a period of health concerns; low vitality; should go for regular tests or check-ups at this time (time this island using the timing gauge for the Life Line)

(e) Gynaecological worries; possible hysterectomy or hernia

(f) A star formation on the Girdle of Venus: a risk of sexually transmitted infections

Other signs of health concerns
Weight problems

People who gain significant excess weight will see this reflected in the thickness of the lower phalange. Overweight people will have larger lower phalanges (even if the fingers are naturally slim), and this could indicate a propensity to comfort-eat. Those who have battled with their weight since childhood will also show a puffiness on the lower phalange on the other side of the hand, and above the knuckles there will be a raised padded area.

When the lower phalanges are pinched, or they are faint or missing on a print, this is a sign that we need a better diet. It may be that we are not getting enough nourishment or are fussy eaters. Check other signs for lack of physical energy.

Gout

This is shown on a print by the tip of the index finger curving towards the middle finger.

Spinal, neck or general back problems

Different palmists have used various different ways to assess spine and back problems. Malcolm Wright reads the Life Line from top to bottom as an indicator of the full length of our spine (for example, islands at the lower end of the line will show lower back problems). Some palmists consider the Fate Line an important measure of the spine. Keep these ideas in mind when assessing a palm, and see which best fits your own experience.

The middle finger, particularly if curved or missing on a print, can hint at possible back problems or spinal damage.

Prostate gland problems

A curved, almost bent, top section of the inside of the little finger can indicate prostate gland problems.

Remember the two-fold application of lines. For example, an island at the begining of the Life Line can indicate either a period of weak health in our youth or a feeling of being misunderstood or unsupported in the childhood and teenage years. A star on the Head Line can indicate illnesses related to high blood pressure at a particular age or it can indicate a project we launch that becomes an unexpected success.

Palm Print 37
Signs of prostate gland problems.

This is shown by a curved top section of the inside of the little finger

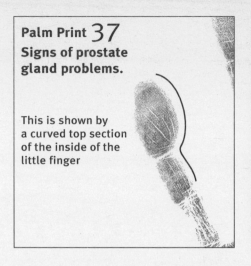

Our hand shape can warn of potential health worries due to the following:

Fire: burnout, accidents (as a result of speed, recklessness or impetuosity)

Earth: weight gain, fatigue, stress

Air: headaches, colds, wrong diet, allergies, nervous tension, mental fatigue

Water: addiction, allergies, breakdown, negativity

Palm Print 38
Signs of heart problems

Palm Print B was taken six years after Palm Print A and coincides with a deterioration of the heart

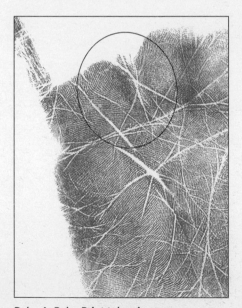

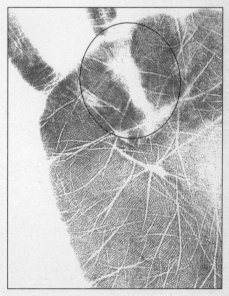

Palm A Palm Print taken in 1993

Palm B The same palm printed in 1999

Heart problems

If someone has heart problems we may find that part of the print is missing directly under the ring finger. However, this sign must be regarded with caution, and you should look for other signs to back it up.

A greater chance of heart problems due to hereditary factors can be found on those with a Simian Line, particularly where the apex is higher (see Palm Print 39).

According to Lori Reid we should also look for shell-shaped nails, a break in the Heart Line, the gradual clubbing of the finger tips and arch finger prints as signs of heart problems. Hand analyst Dr. Eugene Scheimann has noted the formation of nodules under the skin above the Heart Line beneath the ring finger.

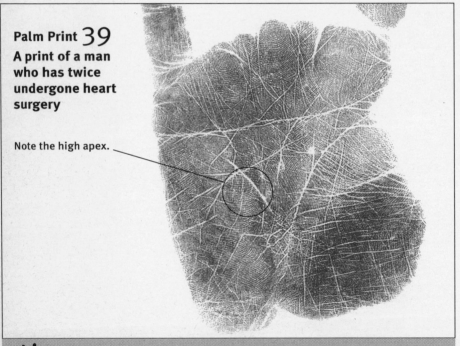

Palm Print 39
A print of a man who has twice undergone heart surgery

Note the high apex.

Dr John Manning of the University of Liverpool School of Biological Sciences found that men who have an index finger of equal or greater length than their ring finger are more at risk of cardiovascular problems in early adult life. Longer ring fingers on men's hands, however, correlate to higher levels of testosterone, which is known to protect against heart disease.

Migraine

Migraine is shown by a series of dots on the Head Line (see page 124).

Fertility

Research suggests that men with symmetrical hands (in terms of finger length) and long ring fingers are more fertile (as a result of high levels of testosterone – see also signs of depression on pages 167–9). John Manning at the University of Liverpool declared, 'Digit asymmetry predicts the number of sperm per ejaculate. The more asymmetry, the fewer sperm.'

The opposite is true for women, who are more fertile if their index finger is dominant. (A long index finger is thought to develop due to high levels of oestrogen and luteinising hormone, essential hormones for female reproduction.)

A weak or vulnerable immune system

This can be shown by the String of Pearls effect, which is where the palm pattern breaks up into smaller segments. It can be a sign of alcohol abuse, recent poisoning or an attack on the immune system. It shows that the body is still in recovery mode.

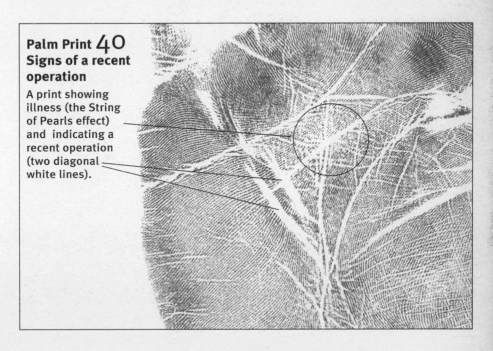

**Palm Print 40
Signs of a recent operation**

A print showing illness (the String of Pearls effect) and indicating a recent operation (two diagonal white lines).

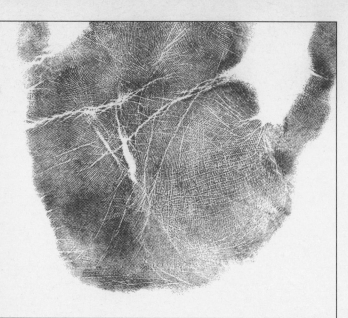

Palm Print 41

Signs of illness and an operation

Note the two white diagonal lines. The patient was also told that she needed to 'breathe better'. This is shown by the Heart Line not extending up towards the index finger.

Drug abuse and sensitivity to chemicals

Drug addicts often have lines that appear faded. This can be seen just by looking at the hand (no print is necessary). Other signs of drug-taking or dependency will show more vividly on a print, and we can often see a doubling-up of the major lines.

The Allergy Line (which can double up as the Matriarch Line, see page 155) reveals an adverse, often extreme reaction to certain foods, drugs and chemicals. If the Girdle of Venus is also present, this is a sign that we must avoid escaping into the realm of drugs or a fantasyland and should certainly avoid taking hard drugs, for we have the potential to be an addictive personality. Rather than see this as a psychological weakness, we should consider it a medical condition. Our senses can also be dulled by stimulants. We may have extreme physical reactions to tobacco and have strong allergic reactions (and at some stage may delve into alternative remedies and homeopathy).

Note that when a part of a palm print is missing on the Heart Line under the ring finger this can be a sign of recent flu or lung trouble. Often smokers will have a missing print in this section, and their health is at greater risk if they also have an Allergy Line. It can also indicate sensitivity in a woman's breast, with the missing part of the print showing up in the corresponding hand.

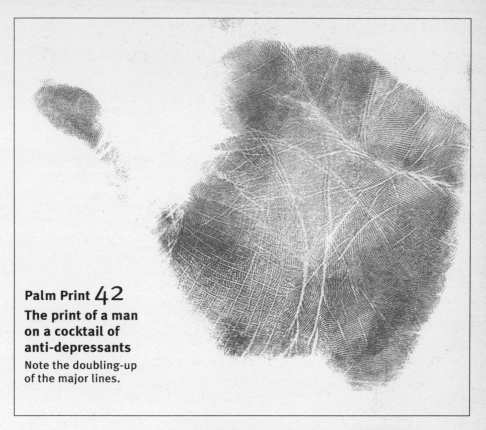

Palm Print 42
The print of a man on a cocktail of anti-depressants
Note the doubling-up of the major lines.

Palm Print 43
A palm print showing two different types of Allergy Line

Eye problems

A large island on the Heart Line is often cited as an indicator of eye problems, but I have never found this to be the case. What I have observed, however, is that a large island formation at the end of the Head Line can reveal severe deterioration of the eye sight or other eye problems. It cannot be timed but we should be aware of when the formation begins to appear and which eye it will affect most (left eye = left hand).

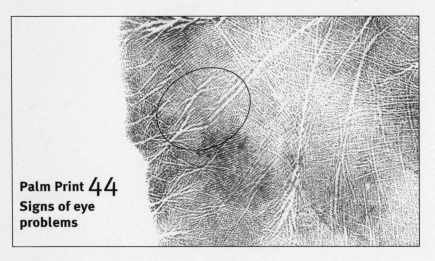

Palm Print 44
Signs of eye problems

Stress, depression and an inability to cope

Stress from work or family demands can lead to negative thoughts and anxiety about the past, present and future. On-going anxiety leads to depression, which in turn may lead to aggression, apathy, loss of self-esteem or an inability to cope with everyday matters. Symptoms of stress can be directly physical (loss of appetite, high blood pressure, sweating) and emotional (fear, lack of focus, irritability). However, the effects on us can vary with age and experience. What seems daunting to us at 20 may not be as frightening at 30. At some point we have all thought that we couldn't get through a difficult situation, but the simple fact that we're still here today proves that we could.

In palmistry the Head Line is indicative of our mental health. If we have any of the signs shown in Diagram 17 on our hands, we should consider doing some or all of the following: talk to trusted friends, try to stop needing to please others, avoid comparisons, express our emotions, set realistic targets, tackle assignments piece by piece, and understand which situations cause us worry.

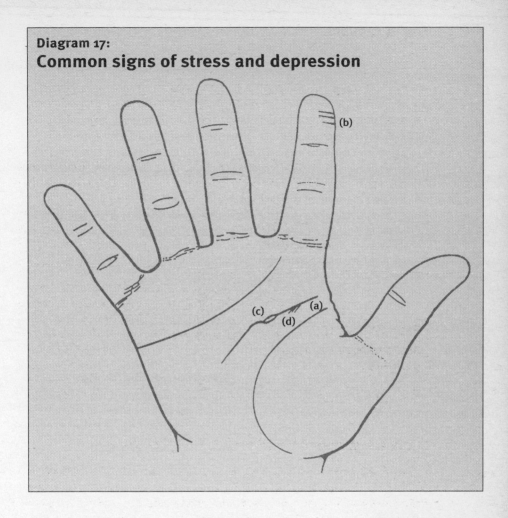

Diagram 17:
Common signs of stress and depression

Common signs of stress and depression

The most common signs include the following. The letters refer to Diagram 17.

a. Sloping feather lines off the Head Line. These are signs of depression at this time (using the Head Line timing gauge).

b. Horizontal lines on the finger tips. These show stress and frustration, often a result of not being in the right job or relationship.

c. The Head Line humps up below the middle finger or dives down into the palm at this point. This is a strong sign of depression.

d. Island on the Head Line. We may crack under pressure and are prone to stress, depression or breakdown. We should avoid competitive environments and stressful jobs. Examples of islands on palm prints can be seen on pages 132–3 (Antonia) and 148–9 (Rosalind). For more details see page 108.

- **Long ring finger:** Scientists at the University of Liverpool have found evidence to suggest thatmen whose ring fingers are longer than their index fingers are more at risk of suffering from depression (as a result of high levels of testosterone, which is said to affect the length of the ring finger). When the index finger is of equal or greater length, a more cheerful disposition can be expected. This conflicts with conventional wisdom in palmistry, which holds that the long ring finger is a sign of a positive outlook. I believe that if we have a long ring finger we rely too heavily upon – and are often swayed by – the opinions of others. Those of us with a longer ring finger are more affected by acclaim and criticism than are those with long index fingers.

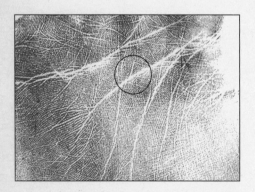

Palm Print 45
Signs of personal stress

The Head Line with two lower islands indicates personal stress or complications. (Note that when the island is an 'upper' island we are more likely to have stress worries at work.)

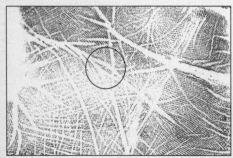

Palm Print 46
Signs of stress over a long period

This print has a Head Line with large island. It belongs to a woman who spent ten years with a destructive, possessive partner. (The print is of her left hand.)

At a palm class I taught a few years back we looked at a recent print of singer Mariah Carey, which revealed a significant dip in her Head Line under the middle finger. The hump would come into full effect in her mid-30s, although it plays a critical role in her psychological make-up. Signs of depression and stress were reported in the summer of 2001, when Carey, 31, was alleged to have suffered a breakdown.

Other important signs of stress and depression

- **The centre part of a print is missing:** we do not like to deal with life's problems and can be vague or elusive when forced to confront them.

- **The major palm lines are weak, broken or noticeably thin:** The palm may be robust but the lines betray that we are currently facing great obstacles. We may wish to hide ourselves away from the harsh reality of life.

- **Bar lines cross the Head Line:** these are times when interference from others causes tension.

- **A fuzzy Head Line (particularly on a print):** we have great sensitivity but also suffer from forgetfulness or a lack of mental clarity at present.

- **A break or overlap in the Head Line:** often a good sign, but when the new line falters then recent adjustments may take their toll. Look for fine, horizontal supporting hair lines underneath this part of the Head Line.

A Measure of Energy

We all need energy to enjoy our lives and interact with the people we meet along the way. Here are signs that show the measure of our vitality in all areas of our lives.

- **Hand shape:** with a Fire or Earth hand we are particularly energetic, but the energy levels of those of us with Air (nervous energy) or Water (emotional energy) hands tend to fluctuate.

- **Strong lines:** strong lines on the hand are signs of powerful energy, vigour and vitality, particularly when the Life Line is strong and curves deeply into the hand. A strong Life Line is a sign of strong sexual stamina, an aura of potency and a healthy appetite for life. (See pages 50–2.)

- **A Mars Line:** (see pages 130 and 133 for examples.) This is a wonderful indication of our inner fighting spirit, quick recuperative powers, battling temperament and strong resistance to disease. This combative nature makes us hard to live with, but we have the necessary mettle to take on any passing illness – or opponent – and usually win hands down. Colds, flu and other ailments can knock us down for a short while only. Notice when this line appears (see 'Timing Techniques', pages 105–38) – these are the times we have the extra strength to conquer illness and fatigue, and they may coincide with times when we need all the strength we can muster.

- **Spatulate finger tips:** those of us with spatulate-shaped finger tips (see page 101) are sporting types who love exercise, fresh air and the freedom to move around.

- **A large base to the hand (at the wrist):** this is a sure sign of an athlete. If our hand is dominated by a large lower section of the palm, we direct this strength physically rather than intellectually. If we also have strong lower (base) phalanges of the fingers we could be known as sexual athletes.

Signs of a lack of energy or a weak constitution

- Islands in the Life Line, particularly at the beginning and end of the line.

- A thin Life Line or short Life Line. The latter is a sign of giving up, for example not having the courage to get back into the workforce.

- When the Life Line ends in one or a series of fine delicate lines, this is a warning that we need to continue to exercise in moderation and keep active both physically and mentally.

Signs of tiredness

Tiredness and insomnia can have a number of practical causes (such as discomfort in bed, caffeine, bad eating habits) or psychosomatic causes (such as anxiety, stress, frustration, depression, overwork). Signs on the hand that indicate we need more sleep and rest are fine vertical lines on the phalanges and a faint-looking print.

Palm Print 47
Signs of tiredness
Fine vertical lines on
the phalanges indicate
that we need more sleep
and rest.

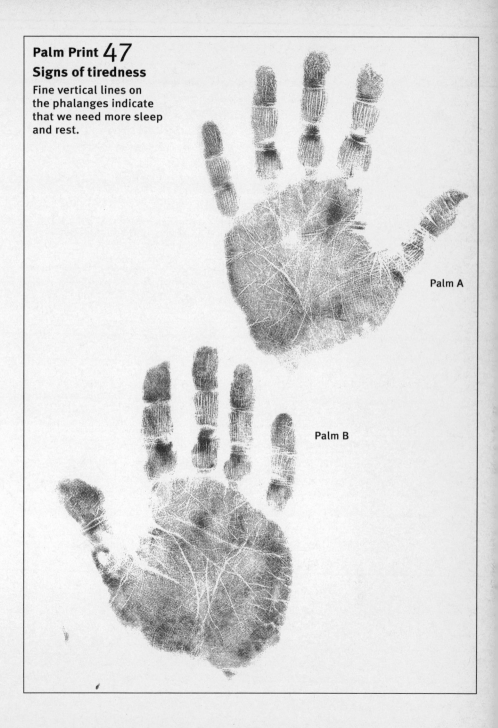

Palm A

Palm B

Money, Leadership and Career

The Money-makers

As everything in the palm is relative to our expectations, background, character, reaction to life and current circumstances, a line indicating money improvements is simply relative to what we are financially worth at that particular time or to our general attitude to wealth. How much money would make a significant difference to our standard of living? A lucky win of £5000 might change our life considerably, but would a loss or gain of a million dollars mean as much to a business tycoon? A financial improvement could either enhance or spell disaster for our social life, our relationships and our current field of work. In order to gauge the true effects of 'money lines' in the hand, as well as key money-making personality traits, we must look at character, reactions to money and the current financial position. All this can be seen in the hands.

There is a great difference between businessmen on a middle level and the real financial entrepreneurs and successful capitalists. The real millionaires are now considered to be those men and women who have over $25 million of assets. When looking at the hand, we find that the super-rich don't often have markings showing meanness or a gambling instinct, as they are rarely the ones who count the pennies and save the dimes. They are men and women with big dreams, determination, obsessions (often with cleanliness) and extreme personality traits and illnesses (including depression).

Diagram 18:
The Money-makers

•Stars: lucky signs showing windfalls or inheritances (on ring finger) or opportunities from influential people (on index finger)

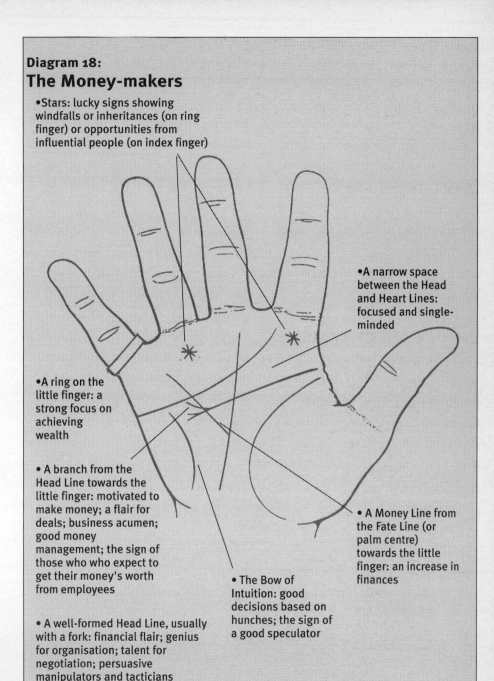

•A narrow space between the Head and Heart Lines: focused and single-minded

•A ring on the little finger: a strong focus on achieving wealth

• A branch from the Head Line towards the little finger: motivated to make money; a flair for deals; business acumen; good money management; the sign of those who who expect to get their money's worth from employees

• A well-formed Head Line, usually with a fork: financial flair; genius for organisation; talent for negotiation; persuasive manipulators and tacticians

• The Bow of Intuition: good decisions based on hunches; the sign of a good speculator

• A Money Line from the Fate Line (or palm centre) towards the little finger: an increase in finances

Signs of the money-maker

The main signs of the money-maker are shown in Diagram 18, but the following are also important features found on the hands of money-makers and top-level entrepreneurs.

- **Strong major lines:** these reveal drive and energy.

- **Small hands:** an ability to see the larger picture and move fast.

- **The fingers look the same length:** money managers and bankers often have Earth hands where the fingers appear to be of similar length, even the little finger.

- **Finger position:** when the fingers are held close together we don't make our money by risk or gambling.

- **The length of the Head Line:** the longer the Head Line the more we can bide our time until the right offer appears. (Sensitivity pads on the fingers – or a Bow of Intuition (page 173) – can help us gauge the right time for the deal.) If the Head Line is too long we may 'miss the boat' entirely due to vacillation or an inability to take the plunge.

- **The relative length of the index and ring fingers:** with a longer index finger we may pursue money for the power and influence it brings, but with a longer ring finger we seek fame, acclaim and glory.

- **A Simian Line, whorls or a ring on the index finger or thumb:** this shows an intense, single-minded focus in the pursuit of money or power. We need to control matters.

- **Bizarre signs and unusual line formations:** we can expect to find some strange markings on the hands of super-rich people. Research shows that, whether the individual is introverted or extroverted, there is an eccentricity common in the super-rich, with strange fetishes, obsessions (particularly with germs) and phobias. So look out for strangely shaped Head Lines.

- **Triangles formed by major and minor lines in the hand:** these are traditionally a sign of fortune and luck.

Hand shape and money

How do we like to make and spend money? The shape of our hands can indicate the answers.

Fire

Fire hands can make big money fast, spend it quickly and be flat broke – all by the age of 25! But give them acclaim, glory, attention and power, and they'll want to hold on to these more. They'll buy status symbols, designer labels and attention-grabbing accessories. Many Fire hands will walk away from financial security rather than face stagnation or bureaucratic red tape. They can best make their money where the commodity is their talent or personality, such as by being agents, promoters, salespeople and performers.

Earth

Earth types expect to earn money the hard way – through application, dedication, long hours and plain hard work. They'll usually spend money carefully and make wise investments; money will be spent on building an extension to their home or on a prized collection, rather than on impulse buys or items such as paintings, for example, that are out of place with their surroundings.

Air

Air types have little idea about money and prefer to let others handle their affairs. They live in the world of imagination, ideas and concepts – and at times need to be reminded to market these ideas to keep themselves financially afloat. They'll spend money on books, gadgets and paying off telephone bills. They can make it big with innovative ideas, designs and time-saving inventions, but should either make the effort to learn money management and business or hand over their affairs to a trusted adviser with an Earth hand!

Water

Water hands can be surprisingly money-orientated, particularly if the Head Line is straight. They can make money on the stock market or anywhere that requires following hunches. They can earn a living working with people – advising, listening and inspiring others. They'll spend their money on keeping their lives harmonious and stress-free, and will buy relaxing music and holidays in the sun. They can be shopaholics when they are depressed, being keen to indulge in retail therapy.

The little finger and money

Our little fingers reveal much about our attitude to finance. The middle phalange of the little finger shows the extent of our capability to manage our financial and business affairs. The fuller and longer this section, the better we are at personal organisation and self-management. A short or flat section suggests that we cannot organise ourselves and should consider appointing trusted advisers to handle our affairs. *Short middle sections on all four fingers should be a warning not to get involved in the cut and thrust of everyday business.* We may wish to be in control of our careers, but should either learn the ropes of business or work on promotion, ideas or product design rather than finances. A twisted little finger (when not broken or arthritic) is a key to a shrewd nature, but often we are not as above-board as others and have fewer scruples. When the top phalange of the little finger is long and pointed, we can make money from our writing and lectures, particularly if they involve self-help or inspirational ideas (see page 190).

Other signs of financial ability

- People with square palms are, on the whole, more financially astute than those with rectangular palms.

- Those of us with long fingers can hoard, save and nickle-and-dime others to death!

- A space between the Head and Life Lines can point to recklessness that could expand to financial affairs, while tied Head and Life Lines are found on those who check the facts carefully and research possible outcomes before they commit themselves.

- Long fingers with a long Head Line tied to the Life Line can be found scouring the financial papers, carefully assessing daily stock fluctuations in the markets.

- A long ring finger is traditionally a sign of the gambler, but we need a few more of the markings described above if we are to take this ability successfully into the financial arena.

Leadership

There are many different ways to lead. People become leaders for many different reasons, and many different skills can be involved. There are those who lead by being pioneers. These people are not afraid to travel uncharted waters and are sometimes indifferent as to who follows. They appreciate the respect and acknowledgement their enterprise brings, but for them the triumph or win is the ultimate prize. Some lead for glory and prestige, others for authority, power and influence. Others are able to front a business or a theatrical show by creative leadership founded on charisma. Usually it is important to have a character able to front and carry an organisation – a personality that attracts attention, the talent to promote and bring in business, and the foresight to map out future plans. The most successful leader, however, knows how to do every job in the office but delegates and manages time effectively.

Most people think themselves capable of leadership, yet many factors can come into play when leaders are appointed (for example, body size, depth of voice and height are determining physical factors, particularly at school and later in the playground of politics).

Key signs of leadership qualities

The following are the key signs of leadership found in the hands.

- **The index finger:** this is a measure of our ambition, our enterprising nature, our desire to take charge and be a leader. When it is short and held out away from the other fingers there's a need to prove ourselves and to overcome a fear of success. We are uncertain but keen that others should not see us in subservient roles. When it is long our fear of failure propels us to accomplish in the eyes of the world. When it is long and held away from the middle finger we are self-motivated and bring enthusiasm to our work.

- **A tented arch finger print:** this, particularly when found on the index finger, can inspire others, bring out the best in employees and pioneer new projects – but we need good supporting talent and others who can manage our time and direct our energies successfully.

- **Large thumbs:** these indicate a dominating, forceful and self-determining character.

- **The Simian Line:** this supplies us with sufficient intensity to be successful leaders but our ambitions may become so all-consuming that we forget the needs of those who work for us. This is also the sign of the ruthless leader/dictator.

- **The Raja Loop:** this rare loop between the index and middle fingers confers charisma and sparkle, as well as an ability to make others feel worthwhile. Others sense something special about us, even if we seek the quiet, ordinary life. Often our physical appearance is attractive. We are sought out for positions of authority, union representation or central roles representing our colleagues.

If we have many of the above signs we'll have a desire to take charge of our life and may naturally assume positions of leadership in our chosen field. The element hand type can provide further clues as to our chief motivation in becoming a leader, the type of leader/executive we can be, and the type of work in which we can excel in a position of authority. We should also look to our Head Line (see pages 52–9) to understand our own particular approach to business.

Ruthlessness

Too often the ability to incite fear and to ride roughshod over others places leaders in positions of power – and keeps them there. Exaggerating the above traits can produce a ruthless leader, while moderation and respect for others will be found in the fair boss. Often independent loners who head businesses are benevolent dictators, and may also have whorls on their finger tips.

When either the Head Line or the Life Line begins lower down, nearer the thumb (see Palm Print 52), or if we have an overdeveloped Mount of Mars (see page 42) we must look out for the need to eliminate the opposition or act aggressively at inappropriate times.

Those who prefer not to lead

An overlong middle finger, a small thumb (particularly the tip), an indecisive or islanded Head Line and weakly formed major lines are indications of people who prefer not to lead.

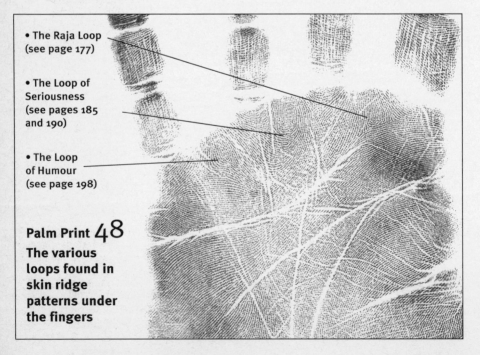

• The Raja Loop
(see page 177)

• The Loop of
Seriousness
(see pages 185
and 190)

• The Loop
of Humour
(see page 198)

Palm Print 48

The various loops found in skin ridge patterns under the fingers

Critics, Perfectionists and Detail-driven Faultfinders!

Looking for an employee with an eye for detail? Trying to avoid a partner who will criticise your every move? It's all in the hands. Check out Diagram 19 to find out more.

Diagram 19:

Critics, perfectionists and detail-driven faultfinders!

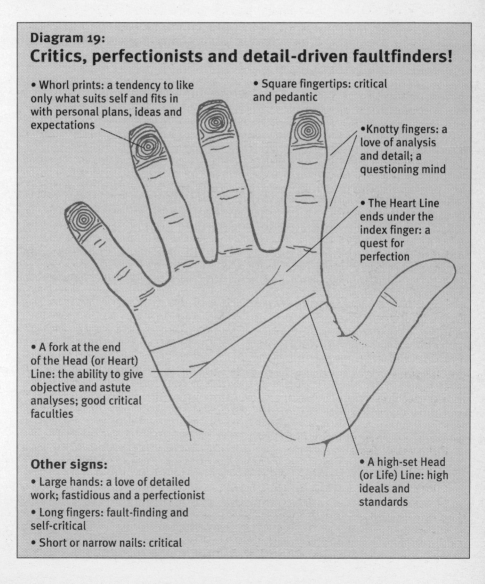

• Whorl prints: a tendency to like only what suits self and fits in with personal plans, ideas and expectations

• Square fingertips: critical and pedantic

•Knotty fingers: a love of analysis and detail; a questioning mind

• The Heart Line ends under the index finger: a quest for perfection

• A fork at the end of the Head (or Heart) Line: the ability to give objective and astute analyses; good critical faculties

Other signs:

• Large hands: a love of detailed work; fastidious and a perfectionist

• Long fingers: fault-finding and self-critical

• Short or narrow nails: critical

• A high-set Head (or Life) Line: high ideals and standards

Making Decisions

To see how we make decisions we should first investigate the Head Line (see pages 52–9). Other signs that reveal particular decision-making abilities include those listed below.

- **Finger joints:** with knotty joints on our fingers (in particular look at them from the back of the hand) we are keen to research, mull over problems and reason things out, often through debate, before making decisions. We are also adept at solving puzzles and detective stories. We form opinions based on scientific observation, will avoid making spontaneous decisions and can be astute when assessing other people's characters. We're also good at remembering exactly how we arrived at our conclusions and would be expert minute takers at meetings! If others wish to challenge our conclusions, they should expect a good argument. We love to argue with, analyse and persuade others. (Smooth joints are found in those of us who are more artistic and intuitive, and who rely on hunches to make decisions.)

- **The Bow of Intuition:** (see page 173 for details).

- **A short Head Line or Head Line separated from the Life Line:** this shows that we are decisive, impulsive and quick to respond in crisis situations.

- **The Girdle of Venus:** with the Girdle of Venus we benefit from strong intuition when making decisions. (See page 145 and Palm Profile 6.)

- **When the centre of a print is missing, we try to avoid facing problems and would rather they were swept under the carpet.**
- **A fuzzy-looking Head Line indicates that we need to find a solution to a problem that is bothering or confusing us.**
- **A feathery or woolly Head Line shows:**
    - **A lack of focus**
    - **A vague response or preferring to avoid problems; burying one's head in the sand**
    - **Bad time-keeping**
    - **Indecision or vacillation**
    - **Unrealistic aims or frustration due to an inability to actualise one's aims (yet)**
    - **Poor concentration or distraction**
    - **A low boredom threshold**

Problems with decision-making

Trouble in making decisions can be seen in the following ways.

- **Large hands:** with large hands we find it hard to delegate and can become obsessed with the small details that so often distract us. Making decisions can be difficult, although we would argue the importance of reading the fine print.

- **Composite finger prints:** these indicate that we can be strategic but are often simply indecisive.

- **A long or wavy Head Line:** this can betray procrastination.

- **A long Head Line that ends with numerous, separate branches:** indecision and dithering can be evident – we ask for advice, ignore it, and ask for it ... again.

When the major lines on the hand (particularly the Fate or Life Line) are overly broad in appearance (almost too strong and dominant), or where a line appears thick and furry, then we are driving ourselves too hard and pushing beyond our limits. We want to get blood from a stone! Often we expend too much emotional energy through reacting intensely to every area of our life, unable to separate emotions from reason. There may be a dissatisfaction with achievements, a feeling that life is passing by too quickly and there is not much to show for it. Of course the truth is usually quite the contrary. Ask others how much they think you've accomplished. You may be surprised to find that others see you as a high achiever. Consider that you may have an impatient, urgent need to succeed (particularly if your Head Line or fingers are short). Look to balance your private and professional life and appreciate your accomplishments.

Look for signs of tiredness and sleep deprivation (see page 170) to back up this feature.

Palm Print 49
Hand print showing a thick Life Line

Diane

This print belongs to Diane, a respected musician, psychotherapist and psychic. A left-hander, her Water hands add to her emotional receptivity and psychological understanding. The Head Line is long, ending in a star with a branch extending down to the Mount of Luna (signifying a shock to the system). Note the large, clearly defined Girdle of Venus.

A whiz-kid at school, Diane was a child prodigy who sang and played instruments from the age of 3. She survived a car accident at the age of 10, as well as enduring misdiagnosis, a botched operation and other medical mayhem between 10 and 18. These events left their mark psychologically (note the star-like formation at the end of the Head Line). Diane has psychic abilities, which she told me were further developed by the car accident, along with a compulsive need to predict the future in order to protect herself from recurring incidents. Since then she has become a high achiever in everything she has put her mind to – but always on her own terms.

Her Water hand and the clear Girdle of Venus are vividly reflected in her character and life experiences:

- A natural musical talent
- The psychological and emotional effect of the accident at 10 and the traumatic death of an inspirational mentor, which contributed to an on-going battle with stage fright
- An all-or-nothing intensity: she quit college to practise her music for eight hours a day
- A need to be the best and achieve excellence: she never eases up on herself or slows down
- Idealism and independence in love: she is considered eccentric and intense by others
- A genius IQ: she is a former member of Mensa
- Regular psychic and precognitive dreams
- A hypersensitivity to noise
- Her return to college to study psychology, later becoming a psychotherapist and psychic: note the Solomon's Ring (see page 142) is attached to the Girdle of Venus (see page 145), suggesting her psychological insight comes from intuition

Note: Her fingers have been shaped by her instrument playing, so the lower phalanges remain elusive on the print.

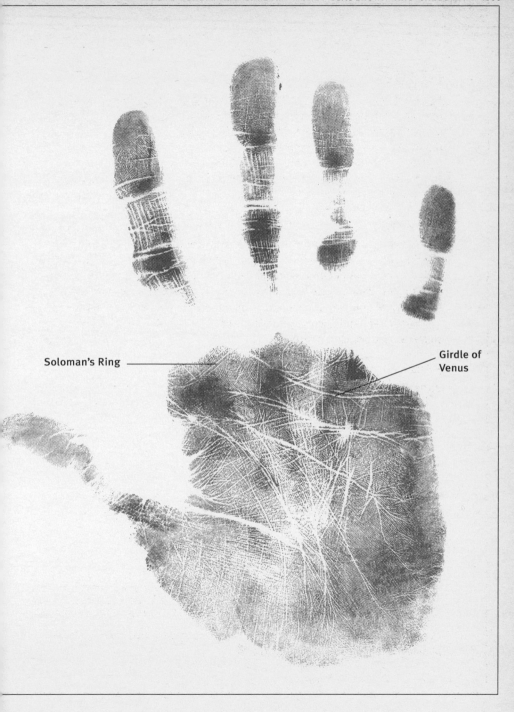

Soloman's Ring

Girdle of
Venus

Responsible Types

Do we see projects through? Are we able to commit personally? Perhaps our company needs a high flyer unable to do 9 to 5 but willing to take risks. Could we fill this role? The hand can reveal the measure of our responsibility in a working situation as well as our sense of personal responsibility.

For an indication of responsible, committed types look for the signs shown in Diagram 20.

Signs of a lack of responsibility

The following signs are indications that we won't settle down into regular employment or relationships, that we march to a different drummer or we simply won't take responsibility for our actions.

- **The Head Line slopes down dramatically to the Mount of Luna:** this is a sign of the fantasist. We can be unreliable, are bad time-keepers and easily become emotionally attached or else resentful if we are not working in our chosen field or getting the respect we feel we deserve. We can grow to resent routine, wishing to be elsewhere fulfilling our dreams (our imagination may go into overdrive at work), but we stay where we are out of fear. We are adept at playing the martyr, too. We can withdraw into the realm of the imagination: our favourite films, music and books help us escape from responsibilities, bills and future problems. At best we can tap into our more creative or spiritual side, and we should avoid joining the rat race in business. Occasionally we may have a fear of losing touch with reality. Look out for an upper

When the index finger appears unusually heavy this is a strong indication that we are carrying too many heavy responsibilities (often the ring and middle fingers will be close together on a print, too). Life may be difficult at present and we are shouldering the weight of others' expectations. As the index finger represents our sense of self, we must consider how many burdens we should take on and reduce these for the sake of our own health and peace of mind (particularly those difficulties that are other people's problems, and those of delicate people who refuse to take responsibility for themselves). In many ways this sign is similar in meaning to a heavy middle finger, but the telling fact with a heavy index finger is that we are resisting these obligations – hating the additional responsibility. See from the hand whether it indicates a dislike of current personal (left hand) or professional (right hand) duties.

Diagram 20:
Signs of responsibility and commitment

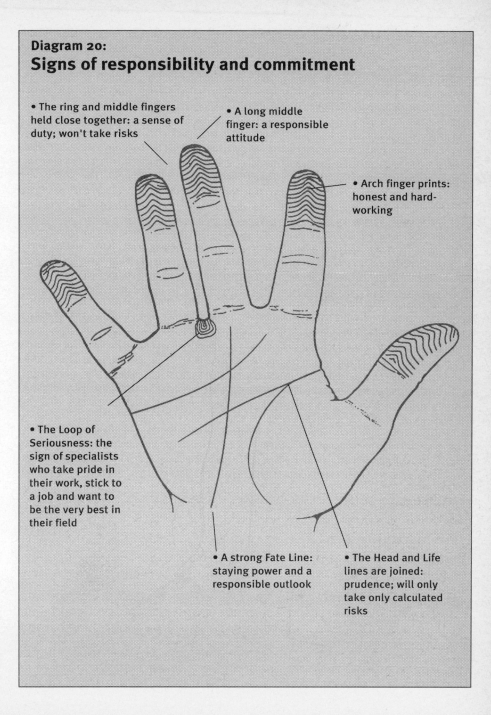

• The ring and middle fingers held close together: a sense of duty; won't take risks

• A long middle finger: a responsible attitude

• Arch finger prints: honest and hard-working

• The Loop of Seriousness: the sign of specialists who take pride in their work, stick to a job and want to be the very best in their field

• A strong Fate Line: staying power and a responsible outlook

• The Head and Life lines are joined: prudence; will only take only calculated risks

branch of the Head Line that lies straight on the palm – this keeps the individual balanced and able to function in the 'real' world.

- **A short middle finger:** we may be unable to commit or take on responsibilities.

- **Small hands:** with small hands we take chances, hate routine and don't want to deal with the finer points.

- **A missing Fate Line (completely or at a particular time):** this can be the sign of a rogue or swindler!

- **The index finger is light on a print:** we prefer to avoid responsibility.

- **Whorl finger prints (particularly on the thumb, index or middle fingers):** we need our own rules and routine and hate to be placed in a standard 9 to 5 job.

- **Index or little fingers both stick out away from the hand:** we cannot abide by the rules, regulations and red tape in business.

- **A long ring finger:** we take chances. If we also have a large space between the Life and Head Lines we should be careful of recklessness.

Eternal student and free spirit

With some of the signs in Diagram 21 we may strive for exciting lives and may not be as dependable as the next person.

a. **The Teacher's Square:** whether or not we can afford to study for much of our lives, some of us have the markings of the person who strives to improve himself or herself and learn new subjects, and also to pass this knowledge on to others. The Teacher's Square is a pattern of crossed lines found on the mount under the index finger (see (a) on Diagram 21). With this marking we can inspire others and often know exactly how to explain clearly and concisely. Hand analysts Andrew Fitzherbert and Nathaniel Altman once wrote that this should be known as the ex-

Check your hand's element type. At worst, Earth hands can be chancers with their eye on the fast buck, Fire hands don't stick around long enough to complete a job, Air hands find the grass is greener anywhere else where once the routine, commitments and expectations begin, and Water hands can be unreliable because their personal dramas infringe upon their schedule, or else martyrdom calls.

Diagram 21:
Eternal student and free spirit

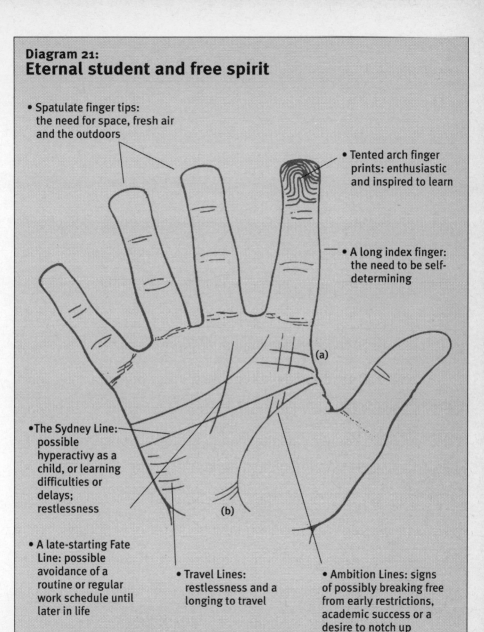

• Spatulate finger tips: the need for space, fresh air and the outdoors

• Tented arch finger prints: enthusiastic and inspired to learn

• A long index finger: the need to be self-determining

(a)

•The Sydney Line: possible hyperactivy as a child, or learning difficulties or delays; restlessness

(b)

• A late-starting Fate Line: possible avoidance of a routine or regular work schedule until later in life

• Travel Lines: restlessness and a longing to travel

• Ambition Lines: signs of possibly breaking free from early restrictions, academic success or a desire to notch up accolades

Teacher's Square as people with this marking have a desire to teach but hate to be confined to an educational syllabus and regulations. If this marking appears on our hand we need to teach those who want to learn.

b. **Branches descending from the Life Line:** where we find lines moving down into the palm from the Life Line (see (b) in Diagram 21 and Palm Print 50), or when the Life Line branches out towards the centre of the hand or curves deeply into the centre, we may have been born in another country or, more likely, will end up living in another country. When these lines branch out strongly but the main Life Line remains the most dominant line, there is a longing to do this. A Fate Line beginning at the outer edge of the palm shows a desire for travel, mixing and socialising.

Signs of Success

The true means to success are energy, spirit, courage and determination. Most important on the hand are strong lines, strong thumbs and exceptional Head Lines. To understand what success means to us personally we should look for personality indicators in our palms. For example, if we're a nurturing, caring person what better success could there be than having a child or working in a profession looking after others? By studying our hands (especially the Head Line and finger prints) we can discover our talents and match these with our needs (the hand shape). There are numerous signs of ability in the hand, many of which indicate creative application and success. Some of the most important are shown in Diagram 22.

Drive, confidence and energy are shown in the lines, in particular the Life and Head Lines. When either begins high up on the hand, under the index finger (or strong branches from this area join the lines) we have a great deal of confidence from our early years.

Check the element of your hand shape to discover what really makes you happy – are you a born communicator (Air), businessperson (Earth), helper (Water) or entertainer (Fire)?

Palm Print 50
**A longing to travel
shown by
numerous
branches
descending from
the Life Line**

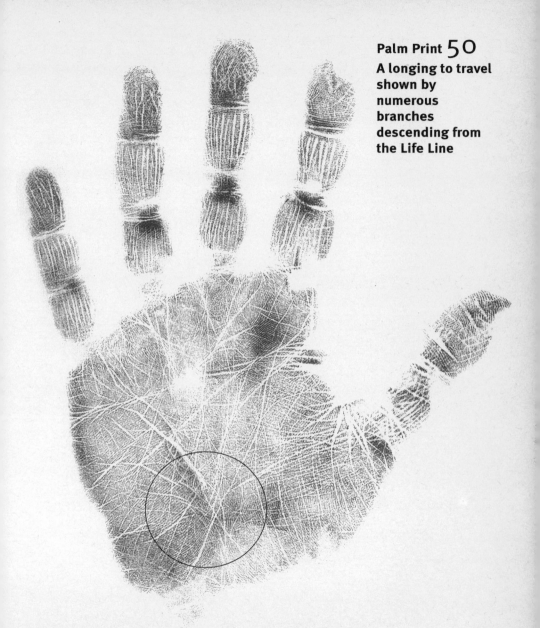

Diagram 22:
Signs of success

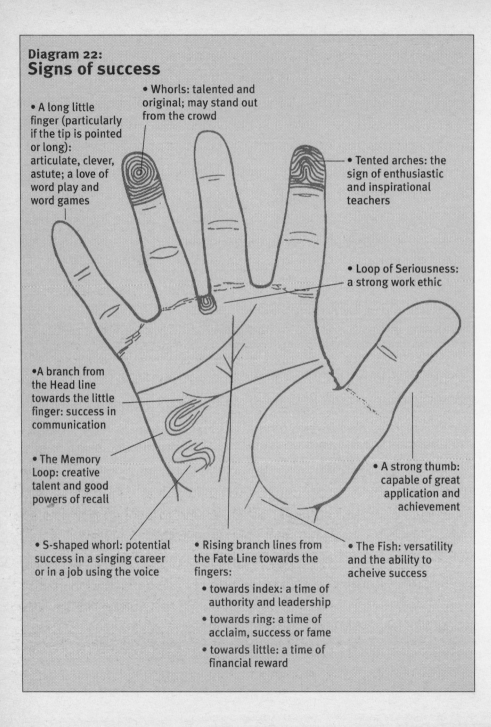

• A long little finger (particularly if the tip is pointed or long): articulate, clever, astute; a love of word play and word games

• Whorls: talented and original; may stand out from the crowd

• Tented arches: the sign of enthusiastic and inspirational teachers

• Loop of Seriousness: a strong work ethic

•A branch from the Head line towards the little finger: success in communication

• The Memory Loop: creative talent and good powers of recall

• A strong thumb: capable of great application and achievement

• S-shaped whorl: potential success in a singing career or in a job using the voice

• Rising branch lines from the Fate Line towards the fingers:
  • towards index: a time of authority and leadership
  • towards ring: a time of acclaim, success or fame
  • towards little: a time of financial reward

• The Fish: versatility and the ability to acheive success

The Apollo Line

Our personal fulfilment and success can be gauged from the time a branch line rises from the Fate Line towards the ring finger or the time when the Apollo Line enters our hands (see Diagram 23). These lines can be representative of marriage, having children, becoming famous – check the rest of the hand to see where talents lie and what motivates us and makes us happy. It's all relative to our personality and our inner drive. Happiness comes when we're involved in personally satisfying and rewarding work.

It has been noted that a strong Apollo Line corresponds to an optimistic, sunny personality and creative talent, but this must be assessed in combination with other factors (such as the finger length and finger prints). The line is more common (but therefore less important in relative terms) in Water hands because of the multitude of lines that appear in this type. When well-marked on Earth hands an Apollo Line points to a practical creative streak, charisma and success with money. Strong Apollo Lines on a Fire or Air hand will show recognition and glory for our efforts and ideas. If we are creative its appearance will coincide with fulfilment or recognition of our talents.

Success is often shown by lines sending branches or lines curving towards the Apollo Line regardless of where they come from, although their source gives us clues as to why there has been happiness (for example, from the Head Line – successful work endeavours; from the Fate Line – our life path brings success, see page 51 (top) for an example).

The Apollo Line usually enters the hand high up – above the Heart Line – and can indicate that the retirement years bring a measure of personal contentment. It is rare to have a long Apollo Line, but when it rises from the lower part of the

The Apollo Line is often found on the hands of people who feel they have achieved a certain level of respect from their own fame and success. (Those not famous, garner satisfaction from the appreciation they receive from those they influence.) There is sometimes a pattern present: they are seen as prodigious talents, and early starters in their field, winning notice at the beginning of their careers. They achieve their greatest sense of satisfaction, however, not through this initial success but from the autonomy it grants them to be self-determining later in their professional lives. I've noticed this line sweeping in from the outer edge of the palm on famous people, including Andrew Lloyd Webber, Steven Spielberg and Harrison Ford – though Ford is famous for having achieved recognition later in life. He has a strong Fate Line starting late from his Life Line, indicating self-directed effort at a later stage.

Diagram 23:

The Apollo line and other signs of success

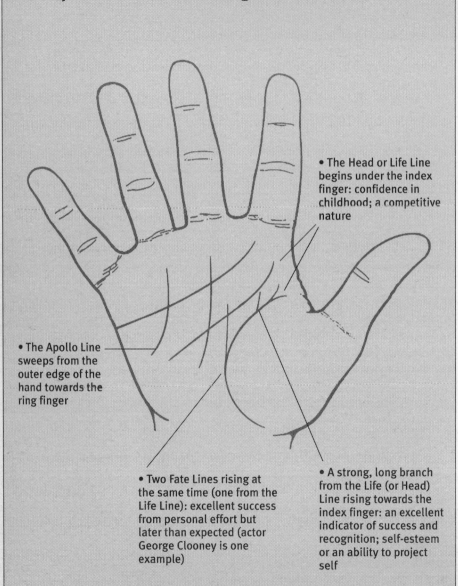

• The Head or Life Line begins under the index finger: confidence in childhood; a competitive nature

• The Apollo Line sweeps from the outer edge of the hand towards the ring finger

• Two Fate Lines rising at the same time (one from the Life Line): excellent success from personal effort but later than expected (actor George Clooney is one example)

• A strong, long branch from the Life (or Head) Line rising towards the index finger: an excellent indicator of success and recognition; self-esteem or an ability to project self

hand we are creative people who wish to travel, go with the flow and see where life takes us.

When the Apollo Line is missing this indicates that, at present, it takes a great deal to make us happy and satisfied – others may be calling us cynical or hard to please.

Two Apollo Lines points to varied creative pursuits, interests and hobbies.

When the Apollo Line sweeps in from the outer edge of the hand under the Heart Line up towards the ring finger (see Diagram 23) we seek public acclaim (or outside appreciation) for our work and have to fight hard for the recognition we feel we deserve. This is also a feature seen on the hands of those who work in alternative therapies, seek counsel through New Age practices or have a strong belief in any perceptive art.

Stars and triangles

Stars can show shocks or a diffusion of energies (see 'Health Matters', pages 158–71), but also spectacular success when in a 'fortunate' area of the hand. We must check what happens next on the line (and what happens on the other major lines) to determine their effect.

- A star at the bottom of the hand can point to an early family shock, creative genius or a flair for innovative ideas.

- A star on the fleshy pad (mount) under the index finger signifies success as well as mixing with the famous.

- A star under the ring finger is a sign of success later in life or a possible windfall. But there's an added edge of bitterness because this may seem 'too little, too late' (it didn't come to us at the time we first

Priscilla Presley (born at 22:40 on 24 May 1945 in Brooklyn, according to the biography *Child Bride* by Suzanne Finstad, has a well-formed independent star under the ring finger. She will forever be known as the teenage lover of Elvis Presley. They were married for six years (1967–1973), but she needed to carve out her own path, first in television (*Dallas*, from 1983) and then film (the *Naked Gun* series) – the latter success came in her mid-40s. In the years following Elvis Presley's death in 1977 she has also been able to turn the Elvis industry into a marketing phenomenon, creating a legacy for their daughter.

needed it, or we resent the manner in which it finally came our way). This mark shows star quality and success (particularly if it is attached to an Apollo Line).

Triangles formed by major and minor lines in the hand are traditionally a sign of fortune and luck.

Careers

There are no markings that indicate we are destined to be a teacher, accountant salesperson, etc. With education, opportunity and interest we can tackle most jobs but there are some signs of particular career affinities, as listed below.

Career and the dominant finger

Index finger: self-promotion, fundraising, advertising, executive positions, motivational speaking

Middle finger: civil service, accountancy, copy-work, analysis

Ring finger: sport, art, music, acting, design, media

Long little finger: advertising, media, teaching

Career and finger length

Long fingers: art, music, copy-editing

Short fingers: finance and trade, management, sales

Career and finger prints

Arch: building, pottery, decorating, self-employment

Tented arch: music, motivational speaking, personality analysis, psychology, fundraising

Loop/Loop arch: media, public relations, sales, personnel management, research

Whorl: acting, speculation, business, science, design

Composite: law, counselling/advice, mediation, social work

Peacock's eye: any career involving risk-taking

Career and hand type

Don't forget that all element types can be found in all jobs, but a Water type, for example, will bring greater sensitivity and personal experience to a job. However, here are some jobs that are closely linked to hand type.

Fire: acting, public relations, sales, politics, management, journalism, sport

Earth: building/constructing, gardening, farming, sport, shop-keeping, business

Air: computing, design, journalism, writing, media, teaching, politics

Water: therapy, social work, nursing, fashion, counselling, art, acting, psychic arts

The Head Line and careers

The Head Line can often give an indication of the career that would suit us best, or of the skills that we can use in our chosen career.

The Head Line begins from under index finger

We could consider journalism, presenting and performing as viable career options. We could sell, promote or move into politics, such is the extent of our self-belief and ambition. This marking can, however, confer character traits difficult for others to tolerate. We have high ideals but should avoid becoming holier than thou. We have confidence in the power of our own mind and thoughts, but should avoid the pursuit of power and influence. Others bestow natural respect so we must beware of taking praise too seriously. We can be somewhat reckless and impulsive, particularly if no part of the Head Line touches the Life Line. Although sometimes eager to volunteer strong bombastic opinions, condemn or judge, we can take others' criticism as a personal attack on our standards.

The Head and Heart Lines are close together

With supporting markings in this section, this sign shows a successful, ruthless, perspicacious and controlled personality. We are driven to accomplish and our self-interest may be apparent.

The Simian Line

If directed positively towards occupations and pursuits backed up by other features in the hand (length of fingers, finger prints and finger tips, hand type), we can accomplish much in our lives. We must, however, be employed in work in which we strongly believe.

A forked Head Line
Small forks on the Head Line
These are excellent indications of talent, balance and capability. I have seen them on people who are excellent supervisors and tacticians. With this type of fork we amaze our friends and colleagues with how many different ventures we can juggle simultaneously. This is often known as the Writer's Fork, and is seen on those able to see more than one point of view and to weigh up the pros and cons of an argument effectively. Occasionally you'll find a three-pronged fork, which tells of an impressive ability to apply ourselves to numerous tasks simultaneously.

A large forked Head Line
This can, at times, be destructive and extreme. Princess Diana's right hand Head Line divided into a large fork just beyond the centre of the palm (mid-30s) when

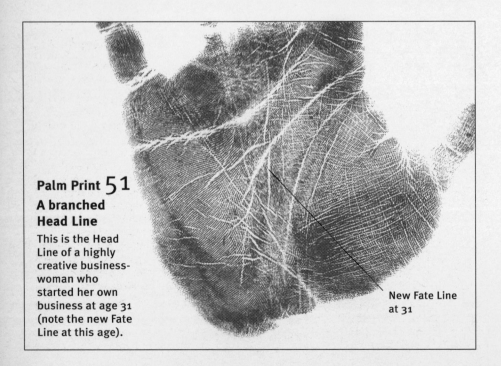

Palm Print 51
A branched Head Line
This is the Head Line of a highly creative businesswoman who started her own business at age 31 (note the new Fate Line at this age).

New Fate Line at 31

she made strides to live a fuller life. But the split points to a loss of control or inability to discriminate. Often people with a large fork are unable to balance their personal and professional lives. Femme fatale Mata Hari had this fork. Boxer Mike Tyson has the same division on his right hand Head Line.

An additional large branch to the Head Line
With this feature we are highly capable and can apply our intellect to almost any job or situation. The people I know who have large branches can turn their hand to anything. Astrologer Sasha Fenton has this extra branch and has written over 100 books on subjects from tarot to palmistry to tea-cup reading.

A double Head Line
This is a rare occurrence and indicates great versatility and awareness of what others want. It is found on those of us in command of our public persona. With two fully formed (and usually separate) Head Lines we have what others may

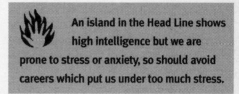

An island in the Head Line shows high intelligence but we are prone to stress or anxiety, so should avoid careers which put us under too much stress.

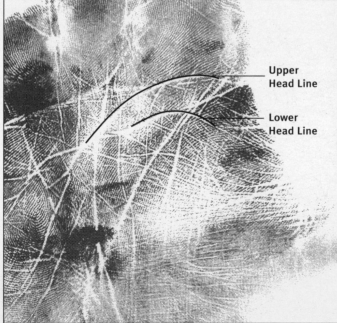

Upper Head Line

Lower Head Line

Palm Print 52
A double Head Line
The upper Head Line demonstrates the cleverness and ability of this complex woman, particularly as it ends with a fork. The second line begins from inside the Life Line on the Mount of Lower Mars, pointing to a quarrelsome nature and a degree of self-destructive-ness.

consider a dual personality. The upper line is our creative, exhibitionistic streak. The lower line represents our childlike, intensely private and somewhat insecure side. We surprise others who think they know us well if we reveal our two very different public and private sides. We are able to tap into extraordinary talents and utilise them to garner attention and acclaim. The famous self-publicising psychic palmist Cheiro possessed two Head Lines, as does the creative genius Michael Jackson, also a master of promotion and publicity on a mass-media scale. Salvador Dali was another with two Head Lines. One of my clients who had a double Head Line began a double-life with a secret career as a female impersonator. Timing this line, it was clear to see that it began at the age he started performing and later joined the main line at the age he went public.

The Head Line and writing talent

Writers usually have long Head Lines and distinctive little fingers. Those of us with straight Head Lines should write factual work based upon our experience. With a curved Head Line we should write from our imagination. With a strongly curved Head Line we could even write drama, soap opera storylines, melodrama or science fiction – but there needs to be a stabilising line (a horizontal branch) to keep us able to work in the real world and to be published.

The appearance of Solomon's Ring (page 142) can confirm other signs of writing talent, particularly if we are writing in the field of self-help or psychology. With the Loop of Humour (page 178) we can see the ridiculous side of life and will be able to write comedy well.

A branch from the Head Line towards the little finger indicates that we can make money from writing and shows the age that we do. A line diving from under the index finger onto the Head Line can be a time when a book is published (look too for the appearance of an Apollo Line, particularly from the Fate Line).

> The Creative Curve (see page 82) is an excellent sign for writers, designers and anyone else in creative professions who enjoys pushing the boundaries at work and developing new ideas.

PART 4

PALMISTRY IN ACTION

A Quick Reference Guide to the Stages of Palm Reading

Let's recap on the major areas we need to explore when thoroughly examining hands. At all times look for signs that re-emphasise a major feature found in the basic hand shape.

1. Take a few moments to gain first impressions of the hands. What jumps out first? The size, strength of the lines? A Simian Line? The multitude of fine lines? How the fingers are held? Test the fingers and thumb for flexibility or stiffness, and feel the general texture and strength of the hands.

2. Examine the size of the hands. Then measure the shape of the palm and length of the fingers, as these will reveal facts including a possible hand element.

3. Determine the ruling hand, but continue to read both hands throughout. Observe the major differences between hands in line formation, finger length and the relative length and positions of the fingers.

4. Look at the hands' tools: the ten digits. Pay particular attention to the index and thumb as these will indicate the measure of our self-esteem and aspirations as well as the level of energy, desire and ability to succeed in life. Note the dominant finger and look for irregularities with the little finger (for example, if it is low-set).

5. Study finger print patterns on all ten digits, paying particular attention to both index fingers and both thumbs.

6. Look for balance in the hand and note exceptions. Do the fingers match the Head Line? Is the practical (square) hand accompanied by a straight Head Line?

7. Begin to grasp the essence of the palm lines – their depth, relative strength, clarity and position.

8. Study the major lines, determining their source, course and direction. Note differences between the left and right hands and the flow of each major line. Are there any overlaps, sudden stops, islands or forks?

9. Look at the minor lines and markings and note how they support the talents and characteristics found in the major lines and hand shape.

10. Note the wearing of rings, the finger tip shapes and nails.

11. Begin to time the hand, incorporating the markings and change of course in the lines – take into account the character and motivations in order to understand reactions to past and possible future events.

12. Upon examining a particular marking, always look to see if the line involved improves or weakens afterwards. This will show whether the situation is likely to improve or worsen after the event.

13. Remember that markings and lines can have more than one meaning. Throughout the book we have seen vividly what I call the two-fold approach to palmistry: markings and lines represent both events *and* character. Every marking (by itself or among a series of small lines) can tell us about a personality trait or attitude to life. In addition to this, with our knowledge of timing from Part 2, that marking will often signify the age at a related event or particular experience. For example, feather lines sloping from the Head line can indicate both a predisposition towards depression and the period in life when the client is most likely to experience it.

Palm Profiler

This section is not about counselling or giving guidance; it is designed to help you practise your new craft and to accumulate accurate information about people and their characters, as well as become more familiar with how life events are shown in the hand.

The following examples are intended to show you how the major aspects in the hand can come together and reflect the life experiences and personality of its owner. When palmists are consulted they are expected to deliver information pertinent to the person's life, character and history. Now we have the chance to learn from the opposite perspective. In this section, I don't presume to know or understand fully each person merely from their palms. In researching these examples it was important to listen to what the clients said about themselves. This is palmistry in action.

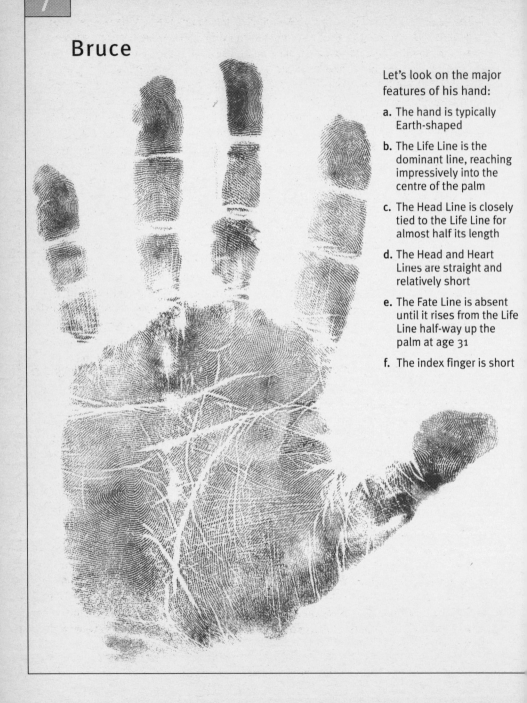

Bruce

Let's look on the major features of his hand:

a. The hand is typically Earth-shaped

b. The Life Line is the dominant line, reaching impressively into the centre of the palm

c. The Head Line is closely tied to the Life Line for almost half its length

d. The Head and Heart Lines are straight and relatively short

e. The Fate Line is absent until it rises from the Life Line half-way up the palm at age 31

f. The index finger is short

This is the right hand print of Bruce, a builder now in his late 30s. He is a sensitive, honest and accepting man who endured a very difficult early life. Once married, he is now happily engaged to a woman he met three years ago.

Even before the death of his mother when he was 8 years old, Bruce seldom had security in his life. His father was an alcoholic who physically abused his wife and children (note the island and criss-cross markings at the beginning of the Life Line). Soon after Bruce's mother died, his father disowned him, leaving relatives to take over the responsibility of raising him. He grew up feeling alone and self-sufficient and without anyone to educate or encourage him. (Note that those who must fend for themselves from an early age are often more independent psychologically and do not possess such closely tied Head and Life Lines.) Bruce shied away from living with his partner until he married, even though he had been committed to the relationship for eight years (c). Bruce seeks a quiet life in which he can be looked after and prefers to live one day at a time (c).

At work he is a hands-on, energetic employee (a, b), but requires much time and persuasion to make decisions for himself and loved ones (the late-starting Fate Line tells us he gets into gear eventually!). When his marriage dissolved (when he was 31) he began to restructure his life and to become more independent. With the Fate Line rising from the Life Line (e), we can expect there to have been a great deal of personal effort to steer his life in a new direction as a result of the separation. The line's absence before this time may imply a delay due to the interference of, or responsibilities arising from, family circumstances, as was Bruce's situation.)

The fingers are short and solid, characteristic of an Earth hand, and they match the rather blunt Head Line, reflecting a lack of finesse with words and action. This is coupled with a natural reserve, particularly in emotional situations (c, d). Bruce's personality is sometimes shy and reticent (c, f) and he seeks financial and emotional security (a). The large Mount of Venus area (inside the Life Line) with its numerous fine lines points to a warm, sensitive man in touch with his sensual side. Bruce is currently involved with a woman who has a curved Heart Line, and their sexual needs complement each other. The relative simplicity of the lines in his hand, particularly the Heart Line, plus the strong upright middle finger, attest to his faithfulness.

At work Bruce adds a creative touch (note the whorl on his ring finger that accompanies the Earth hand), is known to have an impressive memory and can be intuitive (see the loop directly under the end of the Head Line). Interestingly, the Head Line does not touch this Memory Loop, indicating that he does not put his powers of recollection to effective use professionally. Although the robust Life Line (b) is an indicator of his physical strength, the Health Lines heading diagonally towards and through the Life Line point to health troubles due to excessive worry and nervousness.

Cleo Laine

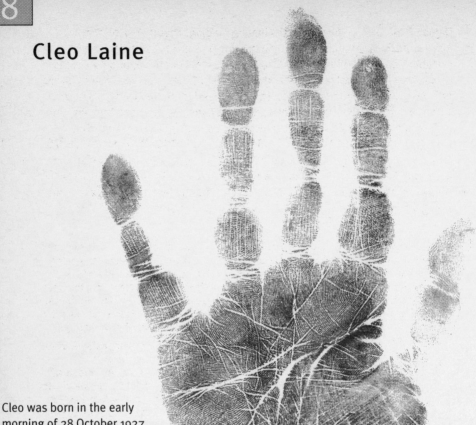

Cleo was born in the early
morning of 28 October 1927
in Southall, Middlesex.
She is a Scorpio with the
Moon in Sagittarius. Some
important years in her life
include the following:

23 – she auditioned for John
Dankworth and joined his
band (the Fate Line begins).

30 – she married John and began an acting
career (the two Fate Lines come together).

42 – she founded a music school and
performance centre at her home (note the
Ambition Lines (page 187) rising from the Life
Line to the middle finger).

45 – success in the USA changed her career,
giving her world-wide recognition and the
backing of an international record label (note
ambition/achievement lines rising towards
the ring finger).

Dame Cleo Laine's palm makes fascinating reading. There are a number of interesting features in her right hand but one jumps out immediately: the closeness of the Head and Heart Lines, which gives her drive, purpose, focus, energy and intensity. These traits have kept her at the top of her profession for fifty years (she joined the band of future husband John Dankworth in March 1951). The same intensity saw Cleo expand her vocal range from little over an octave to a remarkable span of five octaves, earning a place in the record books for reaching the highest recorded note by a human voice. She is known for the care she brings to her singing when phrasing a song as well as an incredible ability to scat (this dedication is seen by the length of her fingers). Yet this award-winning singer and actress has always let her accomplishments speak for themselves. Other features in her hand include:

- **A dominant ring finger and average sized index finger:** Cleo was always a natural performer but admits that she has never been particularly ambitious. The long ring finger indicates the theatricality she brings to her singing (and occasional forays into acting), and her need for an audience. The little finger is smaller than average, suggesting that she is more comfortable expressing herself through song than through the spoken word.

- **The large Mount of Venus and large lower phalanges:** she is earthy, sensual, a 'sexy gipsy' (according to writer Lynda Lee-Potter), comfort-seeking and self-obsessed – soaking up applause for her unique voice and phrasing. With the elongated whorls on her finger tips and close Head and Heart Lines, here is a woman who enjoys her life and does exactly what she wants, regardless of what others expect. Husband John says, 'Cleo's a law unto herself.' Daughter Jacqui describes her mum as 'intense' and says that, 'Underneath she's very warm and generous, but over the years she has learned to protect herself...she's a bit like a cat – self-absorbed and independent.'

- **The strong palm lines and Mars Line:** these reveal her tremendous energy, robust constitution and zest for performing. The strength of her lines enables her to maintain a world-wide singing schedule that would exhaust most singers one-third of her age.

- **The thumb held close to the fingers:** looking at her well-written autobiography, *Cleo*, we must read between the lines to understand what makes this fascinating lady tick – the thumb is too close to the palm to let anything slip by unintentionally. This reveals a highly private woman whom few people know well.

- **Her little finger is held away from her hand:** Cleo needs her own space. Her husband, John, when asked the secret of their fifty-year personal and professional marriage replied, 'Separate bathrooms.' He also remarked that they were still a mystery to each other some fifty years on.

Test Yourself 1: **Matthew Manning**

In November 2001 I had the opportunity to meet Matthew Manning.
He is Britain's most scientifically tested healer and was a media sensation
upon the publication of his first
book, *The Link,* in 1974.

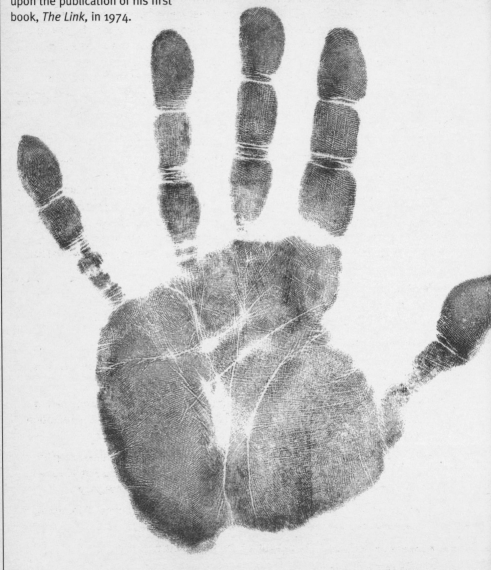

Matthew was born at 4:15pm on 17 August 1955 in Redruth, England. (He has the Sun, Moon and four planets in Leo, and Sagittarius Rising.) From the age of 11 he witnessed a rare amount of poltergeist activity. He later learned he could control the physical phenomena around him and went on to display precognition, and create automatic writing and psychic drawings, talents which attracted great media interest. Scientific testing later proved that Matthew was producing a wave pattern from a part of the brain thought to be dormant. In 1977 he turned his back on the media frenzy and vowed to put his talents to use as a healer.

Making prints of his palms proved to be an interesting experience. Whichever way we approached printing there were certain aspects of his hand that refused to be printed! With certain parts absent, it may be easier to examine the key features of Matthew's hand rather than look for smaller markings reflecting his life events.

One point surprised me about his hands. When reading the palms of reputable psychics in the past I had never found the markings of clairvoyance outlined in old palmistry works, but I had expected to have a 'Eureka' moment with Matthew's hands. But Matthew is not a superman. He is a human being who has been able to tap into an energy force and is gifted in inspiring others to heal themselves. 'I am merely someone who has managed to use effectively what he has been given. I am simply doing my job.' This served to remind me of the words of poet Maya Angelou, 'Human beings are more alike than we are unalike.'

Questions

Looking at Matthew's right hand, can you answer the following questions?

1. Into which element type does his hand fall?

2. He has a contagious enthusiasm for his work and numerous projects. He is also considered a perfectionist. Where are these traits seen?

3. As a child he lived in his head. At school he felt like an outsider and had to overcome great shyness. Even as an adult he hates anger and confrontation. Can you see these traits and signs of his creative imagination?

4. At 23 he began developing his healing powers. It was also a time when he began to break away from a stifling professional relationship with his agent. He won his freedom four years later. Where are these events shown?

5. He admits that he needs to understand new concepts by himself, rather than have others teach him. How is this shown?

6. Matthew believes he hasn't got a head for business. Why?

Answers on page 210.

Test Yourself 2: **Simon Callow**

A few years back I was invited to Birmingham to take the palm prints of the acclaimed actor-writer-director, Simon Callow. (The astrologers amongst us may be interested to note that he was born by caesarean section at precisely 7am on 15 June 1949 in London, which means that he is a Gemini with the Moon in Aquarius and Cancer rising.) This is a palm print of his right hand.

Questions

1. His intelligence and dedication to his craft are highly respected. Where do these show in the hand?

2. Although Simon worked from the time he left drama school, can you date the year in his life in which he found public success and acclaim?

3. Simon admits that he is 'peculiarly addicted to rituals'. He is fussy in his appearance, methodical and needs to keep busy. These features in his hand gave him the tenacity to write a highly detailed, 700-page biography of the early life of Orson Welles, researched and written over a six-year stretch. Where are these traits revealed in the hand?

4. Can you detect his love of reading?

5. After years of celebrated performances he became an internationally known film actor at the age of 45 with the 1994 release of *Four Weddings and a Funeral*. How and where is this shown?

6. Which parent (and gender) features strongly in the hand?

   Answers on page 210.

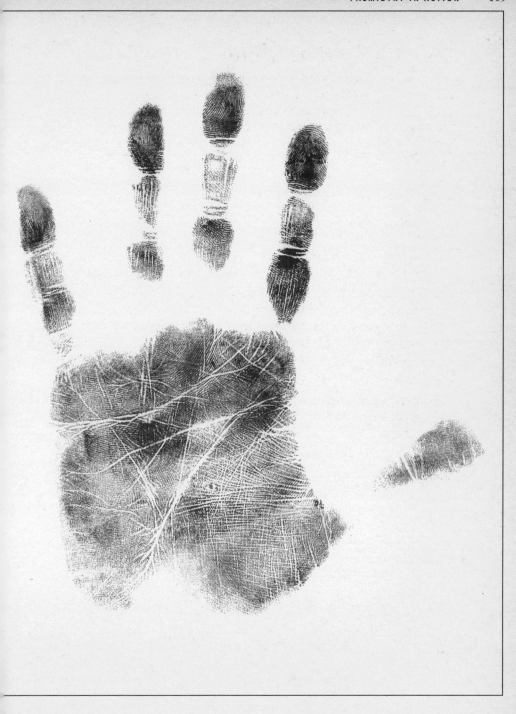

Answers 1: Matthew Manning

1. With the square palm, long fingers and Creative Curve his hand falls naturally into the element of Air.

2. The tented arch print found on his index finger points to his enormous enthusiasm. His perfectionist streak is best shown by the high start to the Head Line (high standards), the long Head Line and long fingers. Note: although Matthew's hands are small (relative to his frame), with his long Head Line and long fingers he is able to see the larger picture (small hands) whilst also focusing on the minutiae of a situation (the long fingers and Head Line).

3. The early part of the Life Line is chained. He has a Creative Curve as well as a Head Line that begins high on the hand and extends towards the Mount of Luna (a connection to the intuitive and imaginative areas of the hand).

4. They can be seen in the rising lines from the Life Line at these two ages.

5. This is shown in the high-set Head Line which begins independently from the Life Line.

6. He has an Air hand with a curved Head Line. The focus indicated by the narrow space between his Head and Heart Lines is directed towards creative pursuits.

Answers 2: Simon Callow

1. They show in long Head Line and long fingers.

2. He achieved critical success and public acclaim at the age of 30 (in 1979) from his role in *Amadeus* at the National Theatre. Note the two Fate Lines entering the hand at this age – one from the Life Line (personal effort) and another from the outer edge of the palm (public notice).

3. The long fingers, elegant lines and extended Head Line suggest intelligence, an orderly mind and meticulousness in his appearance. He says, 'My single greatest shortcoming is my laziness', a comment we can expect from someone who has high standards and needs to work tirelessly.

4. This is seen in the long drop from the base of his index finger to his thumb.

5. Timing the Life Line we thatnotice the second Fate Line rises at approximately 45. At the same time the main Fate Line has faded above the Head Line. A stronger Apollo Line enters at a place parallel to this (above the Heart Line) in the mid-40s.

6. His mother features most strongly. The Matriarch Line is dominant on the hand. Callow was an only child born into a progressive all-female household. An original, eccentric and intellectually ambitious mother raised him.

Life is a Creative Adventure!

Some clients arrive at my office wanting (or expecting) me to solve their problems for them. Others come to gain an understanding of what they need to learn in life and to discover where their life will take them. Of course we all need to accept direct responsibility for our actions – as well as our reactions to life – and, yes, hand analysis can provide us with greater assurance of our talents and needs. But I'm beginning to realise that there are no lessons in life that we get 'right' or 'wrong' – only people to encounter on our individual journey and experiences to create with them. The hands show the choices we have made and who we've decided to be in our lives up to this stage, but the fact that the hands adjust to reflect our personal development proves that we can start over, reinvent ourselves and change our outlook. Rather than wanting to know what the future holds, let's create it ourselves each day. Then we can watch the hands grow accordingly. We won't be able to alter the people (or, at times, the circumstances) around us, but we can change our attitudes to them and be in control of our own direction.

When I began to read hands, I was keen to study many old and new books on the subject. I was fascinated by the special markings that were purported to herald lifelong fame and fortune, and scoured my palms for each and every one. The first time a famous client walked into my office, I was more than a little disappointed to discover that they lacked these auspicious signs. After a while, I began to notice a common link in the hands of successful people (whether they were famous or not) – their hands possessed strong indicators of what I call the three 'D's: Discipline, Determination and Drive. In short: courage. Courage is essential – whether it be the courage to move on, to stay put and stand our ground, to get up when we fall, or to change our attitudes.

Courage + Talent + Energy = Success in Life

Success is a way of thinking. We need courage to channel our energies in order to explore our talents and express ourselves, so that we can create our own personal fulfilment. We must never lose sight of our dreams – they keep us alive. We must always dare to travel uncharted waters, to take risks, to grow, learn and live. Truly successful people (those with fulfilling and complete lives) find a certain balance in their existence; they have a blend of courage, persistence and self-understanding. They are those who accept responsibility for their actions and are unafraid of the tides of change.

Hands show who we are at this moment in our lives, who we have *chosen* to be from our collective actions and reactions in the past. None of us can change the past, but past circumstances and choices have helped to bring us to the place where we stand today. In knowing this, we can cast aside regret expectation and create our future by working now – in the present – on the challenges we wish to experience. And it's never too late to start over.

It is my wish that this book starts you on your own particular journey...on the road to achieving success, personal fulfilment and realising your maximum potential.

May the road rise up to meet you,

May the wind be always at your back,

May the sun shine warm upon your face,

And the rain fall soft upon your fields,

And until we meet again,

May God hold you in the palm of His hand.

(An old Irish verse)

How to Take Your Palm Print

It is best not to wash your hands before making prints. If you need to remove grease or dirt, wait for at least five minutes after washing to make a print. This gives your hands enough time to begin to produce oil on the palm surface and finger tips again.

Equipment

- A tube of black water-soluble block printing ink, e.g. Daler Rowney
- Paper or a pad at least A4 in size, eg. 150g Acid Free Cartridge Paper (although photocopying paper is adequate as long as you are gentle making the print and avoid creasing the paper)
- A small printer's roller (or a rolling pin covered in cling film)
- An oil-painting board (or pastry board covered in foil) or a shiny magazine cover
- A soft, spongy pad or towel (to be placed under the paper)
- A kitchen cloth
- A pen and pencil for notes and the palm outline
- A knife

Method

1. Squeeze out a small amount of the ink onto the board or magazine and roll it thinly with the roller (or rolling pin).

2. When the roller is evenly covered in ink, roll it evenly over your palm down to just below the wrist and round the edges of the hand, plus over the fingers and thumb. Make sure the entire finger tips are completely covered in ink too, and also the centre of the palm – as this can often be deep enough to cause trouble with printing.

3. Relax your hand by shaking it gently and then place the palm down onto the paper. (You may wish to draw around your palm at this point.)

4. Keeping your hand firmly positioned, slip the blade of the knife under the paper and press up into the hollow of your palm.

5. Carefully lift up your hand, without smudging the print.

6. Put additional ink onto your finger tips and place them carefully below the palm print. Then apply ink to your thumb tip and make a print beside the index print.

7. Note the date of the print.

8. For all prints, keep clear records of name, date, place and time of birth (if known) and handedness.

Appendix 2

Tips for Budding Palmists

Some tips and a few cautions to all interested parties...and those budding palmists out there.

- First, explain to the client what can be expected from the reading and suggest a two-way consultation. Remember, the science of the hand is only important if we understand the science of those whose hands they are. Listen to what your client says, what they expect and what they need.

- Palmistry may be a perceptive art, but it's also important to approach the work with some basic scientific methodology, particularly if you wish to begin reading professionally. Question the client if you're unsure of particular markings – you'll learn more if the consultation resembles a conversation rather than a monologue. And above all listen to and note their experiences after the consultation. Build up a storehouse of palm prints, with notes, and don't forget to date and identify all prints. If you can, take the subject's date, place and time of birth (you may wish to conduct your own research into the connection between palmistry and astrology). In addition, note with which hand they write.

- Do not be rushed or bullied into saying something the client wants to hear. Be prudent with your character analysis and any 'predictions'. Although I've found that you can tell people almost anything about their character if you do it with humour, if you venture into forecasting it's important to recognise any possible repercussions before you speak. It's not your job to give advice, just to reflect a client's situation and help them become aware of the larger picture. Reckless, throwaway comments can produce a fear of the future or a fear of experiencing relationships. (For example, a comment that the client has another marriage 'written' in their palms can cause negative thinking about their current partnership and create a 'why bother trying' attitude, reducing efforts to make a current relationship work.) My palmist friend Sally Fry often says that it's better the client thinks you know less than to upset them by saying too much. I've sat jaw-dropped at the boasts of some practitioners (how they foretold a drowning, a car accident, etc.)...which leads to the next point.

- It is important not to 'make' someone's future for them. The self-fulfilling prophecy is one of the greatest weapons sceptics and critics have of any New Age subject. Don't sentence a client to a life of your 'unavoidable' predictions. Look at the future in terms of possibilities rather than probabilities.

- Remember the importance of synthesis – although single markings or observations can be remarkably clear, don't take one sign or marking to be the final word on the matter – ever. Look carefully at the other lines on the palm (and at the overall shaping of the hand) to reveal more of the jigsaw.

- Remember to keep confidences and be respectful of a client's situation and their choices. Try not to judge the life they've chosen to live (and don't judge lines and markings as 'good' or 'bad', either). People choose the lives they have – clients come to us when they're willing (or have the need) to change.

- Most clients seek (and feel reassured by) evidence that you understand their character, their situation and can tell them about their past. Most also need to hear practical 'answers' and solutions to their lives, not generalities. It's important to make life less stark for people. Empower the client, encourage self-determination, and inspire them to have the courage to find happiness.

- Clients can emerge from a reading remembering what they wanted to hear, so always record the consultation on tape to avoid any misunderstandings. This will also help to polish your readings and make you think before you speak!

- Always charge a fee (or accept a gift during your apprenticeship). You'll feel greater respect for your own services (and for me, taking money from clients keeps me on my toes because I want to work hard for my money). Clients will also respect your advice more.

Appendix 3

Answers to the Quick Quizzes

Answers to Quick Quiz 1 (page 43)

1. Large-handed people
2. Intuition
3. Long fingers
4. Earth
5. Air

Answers to Quick Quiz 2 (page 71)

1. The Heart Line
2. The Fate Line
3. Overlapping lines
4. A square box over a major line
5. A weakly formed or chained Life Line
6. A straight Head Line
7. A long Head Line
8. A curved Heart Line
9. The Simian Line
10. An unbroken, solid Fate Line

Answers to Quick Quiz 3 (page 104)

1. A large thumb
2. The index finger
3. A small little finger
4. The middle phalange
5. The thumb
6. The ring and middle fingers and held close together
7. The arch print
8. The whorl
9. A whorl on the ring finger
10. A tented arch on the index finger

Answers to Quick Quiz 4 (page 138)

1. The Fate Line coming to an abrupt halt (usually below the Heart Line)
2. A branch line rising from the Life Line towards the index finger
3. A branch line from the Head Line towards the little finger
4. An island in the Life Line
5. An island on the Head Line

Bibliography

Sadly, many of the excellent palmistry books listed below are now out of print, but here are my personal recommendations as well as those that have been referred to in this text.

Altman, Nathaniel and Andrew Fitzherbert, *Your Career in Your Hands,* Aquarian Press, Wellingborough, 1989 (new edition of *Career, Success and Self Fulfillment*)

Campbell, Edward D, *The Encyclopedia of Palmistry*, Perigee, New York, 1996

Fenton, Sasha and Malcolm Wright, *Living Palmistry*, Aquarian Press, Wellingborough, 1990 (new edition of *The Living Hand*)

Fitzherbert, Andrew, *Hand Psychology*, Avery, New York, 1989

Hutchinson, Beryl, *Your Life in Your Hands*, Sphere, London, 1967

Ludas, Joseph M, *Science at Your Fingertips*, Forensic Press, Raleigh, North Carolina, 1998

Nishitani, Yasuto, *Palmistry Revolution,* Tachibana Shuppan, Tokyo, 1992

Reid, Lori, *The Art of Hand Reading,* Dorling Kindersley, London, 1996

Reid, Lori, *Health in Your Hands*, Aquarian Press, Wellingborough, 1993

Scheimann, Eugene and Nathaniel Altman, *Medical Palmistry*, Aquarian Press, Wellingborough, 1989

Sheely, Gail, *New Passages*, Harper Collins, London 1996

Squire, Elizabeth Daniels, *Palmistry Made Practical*, Wilshire Book Co, California, 1969

Books by Noel Jaquin, Julius Spier, Charlotte Wolff, Mir Bashir, William G. Benham, Beverly Jaegers, Peter West and Fred Gettings are excellent additions to your library.

Some of the above books can be obtained directly through Flare's mail order department. Write or call for a list: PO Box 10126, London NW3 7WD, England. Tel: 020 8381 4169.

Frank Clifford can be contacted at:
PO Box 10126
London NW3 7WD
England

For details of forthcoming seminars and talks, email Frank at info@flareuk.com or visit Flare's website at www.flareuk.com

Index